A NATURAL HISTORY OF THE
ANTARCTIC

A NATURAL HISTORY OF THE ANTARCTIC

ANTARCTIC

Life in the Freezer

Alastair Fothergill

Foreword by David Attenborough

With specially commissioned photographs by Ben Osborne

STERLING PUBLISHING CO., INC.
NEW YORK

PICTURE CREDITS

BBC Books would like to thank the following for providing photographs and for permission to reproduce copyright material. While every effort has been made to trace and acknowledge all copyright holders, we would like to apologise should there have been any errors or omissions.

All photographs by **Ben Osborne** except: **Doug Allen** pages 180 bottom and 197; **Ardea** pages 30–1 (E. Mickleburgh) and 198 top (Graham Robertson); **British Antarctic Survey** page 30 bottom (D. Vaughan); **J. Allan Cash** page 52 top (Martha Holmes); **Alastair Fothergill** pages 11, 52 bottom and 205; **Markus Horning** page 200; **Gerald Kooyman** page 190 both; **Oxford Scientific Films** pages 46 bottom (C. J. Gilbert), 145, 146 bottom (both Ben Osborne) and 151 (Doug Allan); **Planet Earth Pictures** page 183 (Bora Merdsoy); **Graham Robertson** pages 174, 193 both, 194–5 and 212–3; **D. M. and M. E. Rootes** pages 46 top and 52–3; **Tony Stone Worldwide** page 218–9 (Ben Osborne); **Kim Westerskov** pages 186–7, 189, 211, 214 and 217.

Maps by Eugene Fleury

Library of Congress Cataloging-in-Publication Data

Fothergill, Alastair.
  [Life in the freezer]
  A natural history of the Antarctic : life in the freezer / Alastair
Fothergill ; foreword by David Attenborough ; with specially
commissioned photographs by Ben Osborne.
        p.   cm.
  Originally published: Life in the freezer. London : BBC Books, 1993.
  Includes index.
  ISBN 0-8069-1346-0
  1. Natural history—Antarctica.   2. Antarctica.   I. Title.
QH84.2.F68   1995
508.98′9—dc20   94-23841
                                                                  CIP

2   4   6   8   10   9   7   5   3   1

Published 1995 by Sterling Publishing Company, Inc.
387 Park Avenue South, New York, N.Y. 10016
By arrangement with BBC Books, a division of BBC Enterprises Ltd.
Originally published 1993 in Great Britain by BBC Books
under the title *Life in the Freezer: A Natural History of the Antarctic*
© 1993 by Alastair Fothergill; Foreword © 1993 by David Attenborough
Distributed in Canada by Sterling Publishing
% Canadian Manda Group, One Atlantic Avenue, Suite 105
Toronto, Ontario, Canada M6K 3E7
Printed and bound in Hong Kong
All rights reserved

Sterling ISBN 0-8069-1346-0

PAGE 1 An ice cave created by the melting action of sea water.

PAGES 2–3 Dramatic ice cliffs along the edge of a tabular iceberg.

PAGES 6–7 A view of the Antarctic Peninsula across pack ice in Marguerite Bay.

PAGES 8–9 An unusually striped iceberg towers above the 50 foot yacht Damien II.

CONTENTS

ACKNOWLEDGEMENTS

ONE OF THE most satisfying and rewarding aspects of making a series of natural history films is seeing the idea grow from little more than a pin in a map into complete films and, in this case, a book as well. Along the way many people became involved, adding their help and talents and giving the whole project momentum. I was lucky enough to be able to enlist the help of the very best.

From the very beginning we were given enormous support by the various national surveys and the scientists and support staff they employ. In particular the Australian survey allowed Steven De Vere to spend almost a year at their Mawson base to film the emperor penguins in winter. The New Zealand and American surveys supported us in the Ross Sea and even allowed us to visit the South Pole, which we could never have organised ourselves. The British Antarctic Survey encouraged the project from the start and gave us endless help throughout the two years of filming. Many scientists gave freely of their time and without their help the series and this book would have been very bare. Everyone at Falkland Islands Company worked hard to provide us with an excellent base in the South Atlantic, while the crew of HMS *Polar Circle* (now renamed *Endurance*) and a number of the Royal Fleet Auxiliary ships made us welcome and gave us safe passage.

We made the decision early on in the project to control our own transport and movements whenever possible. David Rootes began organising this two years before any filming started and made sure that everyone was properly equipped and well fed. He has also been a great help with this book for which I am particularly grateful. David also found us the two boats which were probably the most important factors in the project's success. Few small vessels can be better equipped than the *Abel-J* which became home for the divers and the centre of a whole filming operation. Hamilton Carter and his crew were endlessly patient and supportive of our demands. Sal Battinelli and the whole of the office back in Boston ensured everything went very smoothly. Sally and Jérôme Poncet who own the yacht *Damien II* have more experience of sailing around South Georgia and the Antarctic Peninsula than anyone else to date. Not only did they allow us to benefit from this enormous fund of knowledge but took us in the *Damien II* to places we would never have reached in any other way.

These arrangements were put in place to support a camera team that had to face the worst of the Antarctic weather. Day after day Doug Allan and Peter Scoones dived in sub-zero temperatures and gathered remarkable new underwater images. On the surface Paul Atkins, Simon King, Hugh Miles, Hugh Maynard, Ian McCarthy, Mike Richards, Rick Price and John Toulson patiently put up with appalling conditions to bring back a wealth of material. Under the ice Mike deGruy and Andrew Penniket were well supported by an experienced team from Television New Zealand. Steven De Vere overwintered to produce remarkable film of emperor penguins. His patience and persistence produced some of the most memorable images in the series. Errol Samuelson and Trevor Gosling recorded David Attenborough's words despite the gales.

The television production team combined a good deal of Antarctic experience with enormous enthusiasm for the subject. Lance Tickell, Ned Kelly, Peter Bassett and Martha Holmes organised and directed filming trips that were enormous logistical challenges. In the cutting room they have worked alongside Martin Elsbury, Alan Hoida and Liz Thoyts to craft strong stories out of a wealth of material. Television New Zealand's natural history unit gave us the benefit of their experience in the Ross Sea and I am very grateful to Neil Harraway who helped produce the series from their end. Finally, Ruth Flowers worked extremely hard to keep us organised, on budget and in good spirits. Her telexes were a life-line and it was always a great comfort to have someone so reliable on the other end of the satellite.

In the past, David Attenborough's major projects have come from his own pen, but for this series David kindly agreed to become involved in an idea that I had been hatching for some time. His presence in the series, his words and the feelings they expressed, have proved a cornerstone of the programmes. I am extremely grateful for David's enormous contribution and for the Foreword he has written for this book.

Most of the photographs in this book are Ben Osborne's. Somehow, between taking the stills, Ben also found time to provide invaluable field assistance to the cameramen. His patience and talent is obvious in his images.

Sheila Ableman of BBC Books kindly commissioned this book and, with the help of Deborah Taylor, Joanna Wiese, Jennifer Fry, Caroline Plaisted and Frank Philips, has allowed me a very late deadline. I am grateful to Judy Maxwell for editing the text and both Ben and I felt Judith Robertson did an excellent job designing the final product.

Finally I would especially like to thank Melinda Barker for all her patience when I was enjoying myself down south and her enormous support as I struggled to finish the book.

ALASTAIR FOTHERGILL

Providing the photographs for this book has been both a privilege and a pleasure and I am extremely grateful to Alastair Fothergill for inviting me to join the *Life in the Freezer* team. I am also indebted to Sir David Attenborough, Ian McCarthy, Mike Richards, Paul Atkins and Trevor Gosling for their excellent company in the field and their positive attitude to my work.

Jérôme and Sally Poncet have provided me with many extraordinary experiences in Antarctica aboard their yacht *Damien II* during the last ten years and I am particularly grateful to them both for their hospitality and friendship and for creating photographic opportunities far beyond those which are available to most Antarctic travellers.

My photographic task was made considerably easier through the help of Nikon UK Ltd and the Paterson Photax Group Ltd. Both companies have supplied excellent equipment and technical support.

Finally I am deeply grateful to my wife, Susan, who stayed at home looking after our young daughter amidst a chaos of builders, plumbers, plaster dust and tea chests while I enjoyed the comparatively simple task of taking the photographs for this book.

BEN OSBORNE

FOREWORD BY
DAVID ATTENBOROUGH

THE ANTARCTIC seas are among the most hospitable in the world – for those, that is to say, that live beneath their surface. The waters are extremely rich in oxygen and swarm with food, both vegetable and animal. Above, the turbulent stormy skies provide highways along which travel can be astonishingly fast and almost effortless – for those creatures that are sufficiently expert aeronauts. But if you are a land animal, condemned to travel on foot, Antarctica is the most hostile and forbidding place on earth. No animal of any size can survive permanently on the surface of the continent, except for human beings and the creatures that inhabit the microclimates that humanity creates for itself.

Those facts, to a natural history film-maker, add up to a most tempting prize and a huge problem. Here are some of the most impressive natural sights his lenses will ever confront: a million penguins on a hillside, standing upright with their chicks alongside, and packed together with scarcely more than a flipper-length between them; a wandering albatross, the biggest of all flying birds, soaring overhead on wings over 3 metres across, returning after a thousand kilometre journey with food for its chick; down on the beaches, bull elephant seals, 5 metres long and weighing up to 4 tonnes, rearing up to twice the height of a man and battling for the possession of females. If you walk out to the edge of the sea ice that for much of the year fringes the continent, families of killer whales will appear and swim alongside you, breaking the surface to eye you speculatively. And if you have the nerve to enter the sea you will witness one of the most glorious of underwater spectacles – great squadrons of penguins transformed from the comic waddlers that you encountered on land into gloriously graceful high-speed swimmers.

David Attenborough and the Antarctic's largest penguin – the emperor.

But filming such sights presents formidable difficulties. The clothes you need to keep yourself tolerably warm, even though they are made from modern lightweight fabrics, are so bulky that moving at any pace faster than a stolid tramp becomes almost impossible. Camera mechanisms freeze solid. Metal gets so cold that your fingers stick to it and are stripped of their skin when you detach them. A small miscalculation about the weather or the safety of a snow-bridge across a crevasse, one carelessly forgotten piece of equipment missing from your pack, can be disastrous, even lethal.

Many films have been made in the Antarctic since Herbert Ponting, with Captain Scott, became one of the first to film down there in 1912. But no one had produced a film, or a series of films, that covered all sides of the continent, from the Peninsula opposite the distant tip of South America to the rather different coast, nearly 5000 kilometres away across the polar ice-cap, nearer to New Zealand. Neither had anyone filmed on the continent throughout the year and the devastating darkness of the Antarctic winter. And while many had photographed the creatures of the air, very few cameramen had spent any time below the surface of the sea, recording pictures of the organisms on which all the rest of the rich wildlife ultimately depends, the vast shoals of fish and krill. Alastair Fothergill, having worked on wildlife films all round the world, in Europe, Africa and South America, found this prize – and, indeed, the problems of winning it – irresistible. To take it, he marshalled as impressive an assembly of facilities as I, at any rate, have ever seen deployed on a wildlife film. The headquarters, on location, was the *Abel-J*, a ship specially built for scientific research in polar seas. Her hull is strengthened to withstand the battering of ice, and her engines have shock-absorbing mountings to reduce vibration and noise to a minimum so that creatures in the seas around her are not frightened away. In her bows, an electronic workshop was installed where underwater cameras could not only be repaired, but new equipment built that would solve unforeseen problems encountered by divers on a particular assignment. Placed thoughtfully alongside it were hot showers, so that people returning exhausted and crippled by cold after long dives could be revived with the minimum of delay. All this gear was at the disposal of a team of cameramen who had the effrontery to butt aggressive leopard seals on the nose with their cameras (in spite of all advice that it was lunatic even to enter the water with such ferocious animals), and the strength, experience and sagacity to swim in the open sea during rough weather and even venture far into the eerie blue stillness under the ice.

Although the *Abel-J* could ride out huge storms at sea, she could not enter many of the shallow bays round the continent and the islands, where some of the biggest assemblies of seals and penguins congregate. So a second ship, the *Damien II*, worked with her. The *Damien II* is a tiny, steel-hulled yacht, with a draught of only 3.1 metres. She, with her French builder and owner at her helm, seemed able to go almost anywhere. Sometimes she took divers into the bays to film the continuous procession of seals and penguins to and from the breeding beaches. More often she had the job of putting ashore and supplying the land-based camera teams. There were four of these. Each had tents, food, medical kit and radios, carried in four colour-coded boxes, and solar panels capable of generating enough energy to power the radios. These teams had to look after themselves for weeks on end. They had to endure violent storms, sitting inside their flimsy tents, and on one occasion even a volcanic eruption. And one valiant cameraman took on the task of spending six months in the darkness to film emperor penguins as they incubated their eggs through the winter.

None of these teams could have worked without the active co-operation of the scientists and supporting staff who maintain research stations around Antarctica, from the great US base at McMurdo, where 1500 people and a fleet of helicopters work in the summer, to the lonely hut on South Georgia where three British scientists live by themselves for years on end. Such people provided the expert guidance and scientific information which influenced where the cameras went and what they photographed. And Alastair Fothergill conceived, planned, deployed and controlled the whole enterprise.

It was my good fortune that, when he came to devise the content of the programmes in detail, he decided that they needed a human figure who, every now and then, would appear in picture, walking up a glacier, clambering down a rocky outcrop, to explain a few of the background facts and, while doing so, convey some impression of what it was like to be there, even if it was only because he mumbled his words through numbed lips and his breath froze solid on his hat.

As a consequence, I had the privilege of reaching, by helicopter, aboard a small inflatable, riding in a caterpillar-tracked vehicle or even, occasionally, on my own stumbling feet, locations where few had ever been before. To convey the reality of these places, and in particular to explain the strategies employed by the birds and mammals that so improbably flourish in them, cannot be achieved by film alone. Written words and printed pictures are also needed. That is what this book aims to provide.

Antarctica was the last part of the earth to be invaded by human beings. They still only exist there on sufferance. Scott, famously and movingly, called it 'this awful place'. But as the following pages show most vividly, it is also awesome, beautiful, humbling – and unforgettable.

CHAPTER ONE

THE FROZEN CONTINENT

I F YOU VIEWED the Earth from space, you would see through the clouds a spinning jewel of blue, brown and green. These are the colours of life. The lucky few that have orbited our globe all recall a feeling of peace, of nature in control, of a welcoming planet. But when you looked a little harder at the top and bottom of the sphere, your eyes would be startled by the brightness of reflected sunlight. The permanent covering of ice on the great white polar icecaps, the Arctic and Antarctic, reflects back 85 percent of the sun's rays. Nowhere on Earth is as cold, as windy or as lifeless as the two poles. From space and in the minds of most people on Earth, they appear very much the same. In fact, they could hardly be more different.

To stand at the North Pole is to rest suspended above a frozen ocean. Beneath your feet there is no land, just a metre or two of ice and then the cold, cold sea. The Arctic Ocean is encircled by the mighty continents of Europe, Asia and North America. Its crust of ice is so thin that recently a massive Russian icebreaker easily smashed its way right through to the North Pole. Powered by nuclear engines, the icebreaker set out in the summer when the Arctic pack ice is reduced to a radius of about 1000 kilometres. The ship sliced through the ice at a remarkable average speed of 9 knots and completed the journey in about a week. Tourists on board paid 40 000 US dollars each for the trip. Only the ship's navigational equipment could tell them exactly when they had reached the most northerly point on Earth. No permanent marker can be used because the Arctic pack ice is always moving. The tourists erected their own north

For sheer size and variety of shape and colour, nothing in nature compares with icebergs.

pole, had a barbecue and played a game of football in temperatures hovering around a comfortable freezing. Several people even went for a very brief swim.

On a summer's day at the South Pole, the temperature is far colder. And beneath the feet is not just a thin crust but over 3000 metres of ice, which rests not on sea but on land. Antarctica is a frozen continent larger than Europe, larger even than the United States and Mexico combined. A massive icecap covers 98 percent of that land, swallowing a continent higher than any other on Earth. All you can see from the South Pole is an endless expanse of flat white ice and the tiny intrusion of the Amundsen–Scott station, a United States research station which is staffed throughout the long Antarctic winter. The ice hardly moves and it is possible to mark the exact position of the South Pole. A simple pole with a brass plaque indicates the spot. Walk round it and you walk round the world.

The polar regions are the coldest places on Earth for the same simple reasons. One is that, due to their position at the top and bottom of the Earth, they receive less of the sun's warming radiation than any other parts of the world's surface. Even in midsummer the sun never rises high above the polar horizon. We are used to the sun being cool in the early morning or late evening but at the poles it is like that all day. They never feel the fierceness of the burning midday heat of the overhead sun that beats down in the tropics.

Their position on the Earth's sphere also means that much of the Antarctic and Arctic have very long winters of complete darkness when they never see the sun at all. At the Arctic Circle, 66° 32′ North, and the Antarctic Circle, 66° 32′ South, the sun does not rise above the horizon on midwinter's day. The length of the polar winter night increases with latitude until at the poles themselves, the sun sets just once a year. For a while after it disappears, a little light reflected off the snow provides a glow above the horizon. Then the setting sun leaves the polar world in complete darkness for half the year. During this longest of winters, none of the sun's radiation is available to warm the poles. When finally the sun does re-appear above the horizon, it stays up for the next six months. You might think that such a long period with continuous 24-hour daylight would make up for the long dark winter. But the warmth the polar regions absorb in the summer is far less than the heat they lose in the winter.

The other main reason for the cold comes from the ice itself. All but 2 percent of Antarctica is covered by it. Bare rock is as rare and precious on the continent as an oasis in a desert. And ice looks white because it reflects back the sun's rays. Most of the radiation reaching the great icecaps of the Arctic and Antarctic is reflected to space without being transformed into heat. With so much radiation being reflected and so

The polar regions receive less of the sun's warming radiation than anywhere else on the planet.

ABOVE *Even today's modern ships enter the Southern Ocean with extreme caution. There are larger waves, stronger winds and more powerful currents than anywhere else on the globe. More than any other factor, it is the vast tract of the Southern Ocean that isolates Antarctica from the rest of the world.*

RIGHT *Icebergs are a real threat to shipping. At times they are so numerous that they show up on the radar screen as hundreds of tiny white dots which in reality indicate an iceberg that could easily sink the largest vessel. It is absolutely essential to keep a look out posted round the clock and many captains prefer to avoid travelling at night whenever there are lots of icebergs about.*

little being on offer in the first place, the warmth equation in the polar regions works out heavily in favour of the negative. Only in November and December, the very height of the Antarctic summer, does the South Pole actually gain heat.

The Antarctic is much colder than the Arctic. The average winter temperature in the Antarctic is minus 60 degrees centigrade. Even on a good summer's day at the South Pole it is minus 30 degrees centigrade, colder than the coldest winter's night at the North Pole. One major reason for this is height. With every 100 metres you climb, the air temperature drops by 1 degree centigrade, and the surface at the South Pole is 2385 metres above sea level. Antarctica is the highest continent on Earth, three times higher than any other. Its average elevation is 2300 metres compared with just 720 metres in the United States. In contrast, the Arctic is simply a low-lying basin of frozen ocean, and the surface at the North Pole is just a few metres above sea level. The constant presence of the ocean below the ice provides continual warmth. Any seal that maintains a breathing hole in the ice knows that it is far warmer in the sea than out on a wind-chilled ice sheet.

Another factor that makes Antarctica so much colder is its isolation. The Arctic is surrounded closely by great land masses. The most northerly parts of Canada are just 760 kilometres from the North Pole. High pressure systems form each summer over the massive land areas of Russia and North America, and spill their warm air north over the Arctic. Like giant night storage heaters, they ensure the Arctic region never gets very cold. Antarctica, on the other hand, is alone in the great Southern Ocean. Africa is 4000 kilometres from the edge of the continent, while Australia is 2500 kilometres away. Even the Antarctic Peninsula, which stretches far to the north like the bent handle of a giant frying pan, only brings Antarctica to within 750 kilometres of the most southerly tip of South America. In addition, the great Southern Ocean that surrounds Antarctica is the roughest on the globe. Intense low pressure systems rush unimpeded round the continent, isolating it from the rest of the world's weather. The warm air from the tropics that is so important in keeping the Arctic from becoming too cold finds its access to the Antarctic more difficult. Antarctica is left the highest, most isolated and by far the coldest continent on Earth.

The differences in temperature and isolation of the two polar regions have had a dramatic effect on the wildlife and flora that survive in them. The proximity of great landmasses has made the Arctic available for repeated attempts at colonization. Animals from the south can easily walk north as summer comes, knowing that when harsh winter weather approaches they can simply walk south again. So the Arctic is home to 40 land mammals, ranging in size from tiny mice to the massive musk oxen. Antarctica has no native land mammals. Though a polar bear could probably live off the numerous seals during the Antarctic summer, it would be in trouble in the winter. There would be very few den sites available and the only other way to escape from the terrible cold would be to swim at least 750 kilometres to the north. Because of this problem, all the mammals that survive in the Antarctic are marine mammals – whales and seals – which can escape to the ocean in the winter.

Similarly, eight land-based birds are resident in the Arctic throughout the year and these are supplemented in the summer by 150 migrants. Antarctica has no resident land birds and virtually all the birds that do occur there are based around the sea. No birds or mammals can endure the terrible cold of the winter in the centre of the Antarctic continent. In fact, the largest creature that lives there year round is a wingless midge, an insect just 12 millimetres long. To survive, most of Antarctica's animals just have to get out in the winter.

Plants, of course, cannot move away when winter comes and so, not surprisingly, Antarctica's flora is very sparse. On the whole continent there are only hardy lichens, mosses and liverworts and just two flowering plants. Most of these are found on the Antarctic Peninsula which, stretching so far north, enjoys the mildest weather. The Arctic is much better provided. Greenland, one of the harshest and most glaciated lands within the Arctic Circle, has 40 species of flowering plants.

The Arctic is also much richer in the most numerous large mammals of them all, humans. Within the Arctic Circle today there are about 2 million people. These include the only indigenous people to live in either polar region, the Eskimos or Inuit, who have inhabited the Arctic for over 3000 years. Antarctica remains the only continent where human footsteps are relatively fresh and still infrequent. It was not until 1899 that people overwintered on it for the first time. Until the 1950s, only a handful of brave explorers and scientists ventured south. Even now the total summer human population is about 3500, dropping to under 1500 in the winter. The vast majority of these are men.

The lucky few that have made the journey south all seem strongly affected by the Antarctic. They talk of a land that seems bigger, more powerful than anywhere else they have ever visited; of scenery that is breathtakingly beautiful; and of a unique wildlife that is perfectly adapted to the harshest environment on Earth. They are united by a desire to return. In an age when over 30 people can reach the summit of Everest in one day, Antarctica remains for many the last place that can still remind humans of their place in nature.

Until the middle of the eighteenth century, Antarctica was a land of complete

FOLLOWING PAGE Some of Antarctica's most spectacular scenery is found along the Peninsula.

ABOVE Stormy weather over Anvers Island off the Antarctic Peninsula.

LEFT As the sea ice retreats, humpback whales return to feed in the calm waters of the Antarctic Peninsula.

THE ANTARCTIC

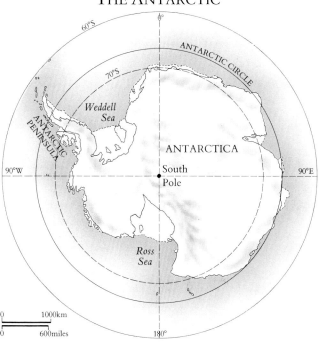

mystery. No human eye had even looked upon it. Aristotle first postulated the existence of a great southern landmass in the fourth century BC and since then, people hoped they would eventually discover *Terra Australis Incognita*, the unknown continent. But it was not until 1772 that a ship set sail with the aim, in the words of the Lords of the British Admiralty, of 'prosecuting your discoveries as near to the South Pole as possible'. The ship's captain was James Cook, who only two years earlier had returned from discovering Australia. He set sail in *Resolution* on an epic journey that would last three years and take a ship across the Antarctic Circle for the first time. In the process, he would shatter the dreams of many. People hoped for another new land like the recently discovered Americas – a green, fertile place rich in gold. But Cook was to find only ice.

Today, most people visiting Antarctica still go by sea. Port Stanley in the Falkland Islands is a traditional starting point. From there, it is just over 1270 kilometres to the tip of the long arm of the Antarctic Peninsula. Few ports in the southern hemisphere come so close but, even so, people seldom leave the shelter of Stanley harbour without a certain amount of fear. The Southern Ocean that lies ahead is the worst in the world. Powerful winds continually race round it, reaching hurricane force several times a year, and huge waves form unimpeded by any land. The latitudes just north of Antarctica are well named the roaring forties and the furious fifties.

In bad weather, the crossing to the Antarctic Peninsula can take weeks. Even the largest ships often choose to turn back and sit out the storm in port rather than battle to hold position in a massive sea. In good weather, a strong modern ship averaging, say, 10 knots can make the crossing in three days. For the first day or so, the only animals visible are petrels and albatrosses which appear from nowhere, hugging the waves with their long wings. Then suddenly there is a change. The air is colder, mist appears and the birds are more numerous and different. A glance at the ship's ther-mometer shows the sea temperature has suddenly dropped. These are all signs that the ship has just passed the Antarctic Polar Front, where cold water spreading out from Antarctica meets warmer upwelling water coming down from the tropics. Each year this meeting place shifts a little north or south but it is always there – a barrier between everything Antarctic and everything from other worlds. To the south lie cold seas and the unique animals adapted to live in them. To the north are animals that, for the most part, could not survive in the Southern Ocean.

For anyone travelling south to the ice, crossing the Polar Front is always a very significant moment. There is a distinct feeling that what lies ahead is somehow more dangerous, more challenging than the world left behind. Soon the first icebergs start to

A change in wind direction can quickly drive the pack ice together, crushing a ship.

LEFT *In places Antarctic wildlife can seem extremely rich. Over 80 000 pairs of chinstrap penguins nest on the slopes of Deception Island, part of the South Shetland archipelago. Deception Island is still an active volcano and these birds are breeding along the lip of an old caldera.*

BELOW *Apart from Man, the most numerous large mammal on Earth is thought to be the crabeater seal. They never come to land but spend their whole lives at sea or hauled up on ice floes. Their total population is estimated at 14–30 million, though their life deep in the pack ice makes them difficult to count.*

appear. They are 'growlers', blocks of ice no bigger than a car that the ocean has nearly eaten away. But as you continue south they get bigger and bigger until one morning you wake to find massive cathedrals of ice floating by. Nothing, no photographs or prose, can prepare the mind for this spectacle. Electric blue to dazzling white, the icebergs come sculpted by the sea and the sun into an amazing variety of shapes. Dazzled by their beauty, it is easy to forget the danger they represent. The radar screen becomes increasingly peppered with white dots, each an iceberg big enough to have sunk the *Titanic*. Even today, the largest of the most modern icebreakers may be crushed if trapped by them.

Captain Cook's *Resolution* was tiny. Its 460 tonnes of fragile timber must have been dwarfed by most of the bigger icebergs. Yet nothing could blunt Cook's determination to get south. On 17 January 1773, the *Resolution* crossed the Antarctic Circle (66° 32′ South) and Cook found himself in 'an immense field composed of different kinds of ice'. He was among the thick pack ice that completely surrounds the continent, retreating and advancing each year with the changing seasons.

With extraordinary bravery, Cook and his crew continued for a whole year to try and get further south. They were finally halted at latitude 71°10′ South by a solid wall of ice. Cook had still not observed any land that might have been part of the unknown continent. All he could see was white to the horizon and he thought the ice extended right to the South Pole. But he was confident that beneath it there would be the unknown continent everyone had dreamt of for so long. He suspected that, if someone eventually did go far enough south to discover this continent, 'the world will derive no benefit from it'.

Cook had managed to get as far south as he did by sailing only in the Antarctic summer. Even today it is impossible for the largest icebreakers to get near Antarctica in the winter because then the waters round the continent freeze over. An area up to 20 million square kilometres is covered in ice, effectively more than doubling the size of the continent. It is the biggest seasonal change to take place anywhere on the planet and it affects virtually all Antarctic wildlife. Most animals feed in the sea and when access to it is blocked they are forced to move north, chased away by the ever extending ice edge.

After Cook's remarkable voyage it was 50 years before anyone dared venture so far south again. In 1819, William Smith, an Englishman from Northumberland, was rounding Cape Horn en route from Buenos Aires to Valparaiso. Violent storms drove his ship south and he found himself among mountainous, snow-covered islands. Smith could not investigate whether these were close to the unknown continent because he

ABOVE *Inside a crevasse one can really appreciate the power of the Antarctic ice machine.*

RIGHT *The cliffs of the Ross Ice Shelf are almost 50 metres high.*

BELOW *A nunatak – a mountain summit piercing through the ice cap.*

had a cargo to deliver. But he decided that he just had to return. The following June, in the middle of winter, he came south again and found the sea completely frozen. Just as they are today, his islands were totally inaccessible at that time of year. He made his third attempt in October, eight months after his original chance sighting. In the Antarctic spring, with the seas clear of winter pack ice, Smith made a successful landing and claimed the islands for Britain, calling them the 'New South Shetlands'.

The South Shetlands remain today the first sight of land for many who cross the Southern Ocean from South America or the Falkland Islands. They form the largest archipelago in Antarctica, a 540 kilometre-long backbone of rocky vertebrae about 105 kilometres to the north-west of the Antarctic Peninsula. When Smith first set eyes on them, he must have agreed with Cook that the unknown continent was unlikely to prove a land of wealth and promise. The prevailing westerly winds are often very strong and massive waves direct from the Pacific smash on to the western shores. When the islands, usually shrouded in fog, emerge from the gloom, they are mountainous, rocky, snow-covered and very unwelcoming. Yet their position on the edge of the Peninsula, the most northerly extent of the Antarctic continent, gives them a relatively mild climate.

Each summer, the ice retreats far enough to release the islands from winter's grip and provide a few large areas of ice-free terrain. There is more life on the South Shetlands than anywhere else around Antarctica. Splashes of bright orange lichen covering whole cliff sides can be seen from out at sea. Large expanses of moss add the colour green to Antarctica's otherwise black and white paintbox. Busy penguin colonies cover any accessible bare rock and the beaches are often noisy with seals.

It was the seals that first impressed William Smith. His reports of 'seals in abundance' brought an immediate response from the seal industry and money for further exploration. Within just a few months, Smith returned as master and pilot to Edward Bransfield. The two men had begun a survey of the uncharted South Shetlands when, on 30 January 1820, bad weather forced them to sail south through a heavy mist. When this eventually lifted, Smith and Bransfield were amazed to see a coastline to the south-west. The midshipman later wrote that the scene was 'the most gloomy that can be imagined, and the only cheer that the sight afforded was in the idea that this might be the long-sought southern continent, as land was undoubtedly seen in latitude 64 degrees'.

The great southern continent, the unknown land, had at last revealed itself. Smith and Bransfield had been granted a view of the very northern tip of the Antarctic Peninsula which stretches up to 64 degrees south. But they may not have been the first to observe mainland Antarctica. On 27 January 1820, just three days before their sighting, Captain Baron Thaddeus Von Bellingshausen of the Imperial Russian Navy reported seeing 'a solid stretch of ice running from east through south to west'. Bellingshausen was then 3200 kilometres to the south-east of Bransfield, attempting to sail round the continent. Today there can be little doubt that he was looking at the coastline of continental Antarctica but it seems he did not realize it at the time.

Bellingshausen continued his circumnavigation and eventually reached the South Shetland Islands which, ironically, he thought he was the first to discover. While moored off these islands, he awoke one morning to find a small boat lying alongside his two far larger vessels. By an extraordinary coincidence he had run into the American sealer, Nathaniel Palmer. Spurred on by the reports of Smith and Bransfield, Palmer had sailed to the South Shetlands in search of seals. On a clear day, he climbed high into the mountains on the Shetlands and saw in the distance to the south a beautiful mountain range. So representatives of three countries, Russia, the United States and Britain, all claimed to have been the first to lay eyes on the southern continent. Most authorities today favour Bellingshausen's claim.

It is not surprising that these early explorers should have come across the Antarctic Peninsula first. It is by far the most accessible part of the continent, stretching north like a long extended hand of welcome. Each summer, the ice retreats far enough to give most of the Peninsula coastline access to the sea and the resultant maritime climate is milder than that of the rest of the continent. This is the gentlest face of Antarctica, an exquisitely beautiful area where most of the mainland's wildlife survives. A series of islands fringing the west coast of the Peninsula protects its sheltered channels and bays. Massive snow-covered mountains rise straight from the sea. Glaciers cut the mountains, calving icebergs into the sea. Wherever ice-free rock is available, there are breeding birds. Whales travel south as the ice retreats, puffing their way through the mirror-like calm channels, while seals litter the icefloes. It is a silent natural spectacle.

The Peninsula contains most of the 2 percent of Antarctica that is ever ice-free, and so is not typical of the continent as a whole. The rest is far more demanding for both wildlife and humans. One of the first explorers to see this crueller face was the British naval officer, Sir James Clark Ross. In 1839, he headed south from Hobart in Tasmania to another side of the continent. His goal was the magnetic south pole, but he found his route blocked by Antarctica's greatest ice barrier. It must have towered over the mast of his ship, being 45–75 metres high, running for hundreds of kilometres without interruption. Below the surface it extends to an average depth of 250 metres. This ice shelf, now known as the Ross Ice Shelf, made it impossible for him to proceed

further south by ship. As he wrote at the time, he 'might with equal chance of success try to sail through the Cliffs of Dover'. But his expedition did discover the Ross Sea which would prove the weak spot in Antarctica's defences. There, unlike the rest of the continental edge, the sea ice clears quickly in the summer. The explorers that would in time follow Ross and attempt to walk to the pole would all use this way on to the continent.

If you sail round Antarctica, you will see, like Ross, mainly white ice. Sometimes it towers over you as mighty ice shelves. Elsewhere great glaciers tumble into the ocean, calving off icebergs which make navigation very dangerous. Most of Antarctica is submerged in an enormous icecap. Covering 14 million square kilometres, one and a half times the size of Australia, it is by far the largest icecap on Earth. On average it is 2160 metres thick but in places it reaches a maximum depth of 4000 metres. Complete mountain ranges as high as the European Alps are simply swallowed in ice. It is formed by the compression of slowly falling snow, each flake pushing down on the flakes that preceded it. The ice started to form 30 million years ago and today about 90 percent of all the world's freshwater is trapped in the Antarctic icecap. The oldest ice in the present icecap is around 700000 years old. Glaciologists who take samples from deep down in the icecap could easily present you with a drink of water made from ice frozen during the life of Christ. If today's icecap melted, sea levels globally would rise by 60 metres, drowning all the major coastal cities of the world. The continent itself, relieved of the enormous weight of the ice, would rise by over 500 metres.

The Antarctic icecap is the loneliest and most humbling place on Earth. From the edge of the continent to the South Pole stretch 2500 kilometres of ice broken, very occasionally, by the tips of the massive mountains below. These nunataks stand like rocky ships in a massive white ocean. Cold air from the high continental plateau rushes down the gradient to the sea causing katabatic winds. These reach over 300 kilometres an hour and add terrifying windchill to the already freezing conditions. Nowhere else on Earth is as hostile to life or, to the early explorers, as challenging.

When Ross left Antarctica in 1843, it was clear that the only way to discover more about the continent was to leave the relative safety of ships and venture on to the icecap. For 50 years nobody dared attempt it and Antarctica was left once more in complete solitude. Then in 1895, Carsten Borchgrevink, a young Norwegian who had emigrated to Australia, ventured south. The whaling industry in the North Atlantic was becoming increasingly uneconomic and Borchgrevink thought the Antarctic might provide new hunting grounds. He failed to find any but he did become the first person ever to make a confirmed landing on the Antarctic continent. On 25 January 1895, his

It may take up to 10 years for the sea and the sun to erode away the larger icebergs.

small boat rowed through thick ice below Cape Adare and Borchgrevink leapt out on to a grey pebble beach. Inland, glaciers bigger than he had ever seen were cutting their way through massive snow-covered mountains.

Borchgrevink was determined to return and discover the secrets that lay behind the mountains. But it was over three years before he managed to raise the £40 000 he needed. He was supported by a wealthy English publisher, Sir George Newnes, who demanded in return that the expedition should be called 'The British Antarctic Expedition'. The *Southern Cross* left London on 23 August 1898 and arrived at Cape Adare in February 1899. Borchgrevink's party immediately set about building two prefabricated huts which became home to 10 men and 75 dogs. The ship escaped when the sea began to freeze, leaving a group of people to overwinter in Antarctica for the very first time. It proved as much a mental test as a physical challenge. The party had to endure 10 weeks of complete darkness, relentless storms and the terrifying spectacle of the aurora flickering overhead. On 14 October, one of the biologists died of scurvy. Eventually the sun returned and the party set out on local sledging expeditions, the glaciers and mountains that hem in Cape Adare making longer journeys impossible. Then in January 1900, the *Southern Cross* returned and took the party further south to Ross Island and the Ross Ice Shelf. From there, Borchgrevink travelled over 15 kilometres by sledge towards the pole and set a new record of 78° 50′ South.

It was a party led by a Norwegian, Roald Amundsen, who first made the journey across the icecap to the South Pole, reaching it on 14 December 1911. They were closely followed by Robert Scott's British team, who arrived at the pole on 17 January 1912. Like Borchgrevink, Amundsen believed that dog-pulled sledges were the only way to travel quickly enough across the icecap. Speed was of the essence since the longer the time of travel, the more food had to be carried and the greater the exposure to the cruel Antarctic elements. While Amundsen's party took four sledges pulled by 52 dogs, Scott's team of five dragged their sledges themselves, pulling over 90 kilograms of rations each.

The story of their journeys, of Amundsen's success and Scott's heroic failure, has been told many times. They were very different men with very different aims. Amundsen's and his sponsors' objective was to reach a pole, and he was determined to achieve it. He had originally been hoping to conquer the North Pole but Robert Peary claimed this prize. So Amundsen quickly changed his plans and headed south, sending Scott a simple telegram: 'Beg leave to inform you proceeding Antarctica'. Scott's expedition was supported by the Royal Geographical Society. Although reaching the South Pole was the aim that caught the public's imagination, the expedition's principal

Anvers Island with the channels of the Antarctic Peninsula beyond.

objective was scientific research. The five men in the team all perished on their return journey from the pole. Scott and two of his companions died in their tent just under 18 kilometres from a food depot that would have saved their lives. The following spring, a search party discovered the three bodies still in their sleeping bags. Beside the tent was a sledge on which lay 16 kilograms of rocks that bore faint traces of fossil ferns. Scott's party had dragged the specimens all that way in the cause of science.

Despite its perils, Antarctica still lures scientists to make the journey across the Southern Ocean to the continent. A few even stay there through the winter but they are trapped. Scientific bases built on the solid rock of the continent find themselves surrounded by pack ice up to 3 metres thick. The enormous icebreakers that supply the bases in the summer are forced to leave, and scientists and support staff are left to overwinter alone. Modern communication systems allow them to telephone or send a fax by satellite. But in event of an emergency, a call for help could not be answered. No icebreaker could make its way through and no pilot would risk flying in such unpredictable conditions. Protected by its ice, Antarctica remains the last true wilderness on Earth.

FOLLOWING PAGE A katabatic wind exceeding 160 kilometres per hour whips up the ocean.

CHAPTER TWO

THE
BOUNTIFUL
SEA

'NAVIGATION IN the area covered by this volume is rendered difficult by a number of considerations'. This typical understatement begins *The Antarctic Pilot*, essential reading for all sailors brave enough to journey into the Southern Ocean. Slowly assembled by the Hydrographer to the British Navy, the Pilot goes on to list the difficulties to navigation as sea ice; sudden, violent and unpredictable changes in the weather; instability of the compass; inadequate charts; and total lack of navigational aids. In other words, venture south at your peril.

The Southern Ocean covers 36 million square kilometres to the south of the Antarctic Polar Front. This is the point where cold, surface water travelling north from the edge of Antarctica meets and sinks below warm water travelling south from the tropics. The exact position of the Polar Front changes from year to year by as much as 150 kilometres. But it is always found between 50 and 60 degrees South, and in any year can be drawn on a map. When you cross it going south, you are entering the Southern Ocean. For most people, and for the purposes of this book, the Polar Front also marks the beginning of the Antarctic.

Sailors crossing the Polar Front know they are entering the roughest, windiest, most unpredictable ocean on the globe. Near the continent, cold winds are always blowing down from the high icecap, driven largely by gravity. These katabatic winds are extremely strong and travel at speeds unmatched anywhere else in the world. They often move at velocities of more than 80 kilometres per hour and can attain a record of

Black-browed albatrosses in Drake Passage between the Antarctic Peninsula and South America.

300 kilometres per hour. On reaching the coast they are deflected to the west by the Earth's rotation. This produces currents going west, often called the East Wind Drift, in the sea near the continent and out to about 65 degrees.

Further north the ocean currents are dominated by the prevailing westerlies. Because there is so much open water with no land in the way, these winds can rush uninterrupted round the globe, creating massive waves. They also drive the Antarctic Circumpolar Current, or West Wind Drift, which runs all round the outer edge of the Southern Ocean. The Circumpolar Current is four times more powerful than the Gulf Stream, and moves vast quantities of water. The Drake Passage between the tip of South America and the Antarctic Peninsula is the narrowest gap the ocean must squeeze through. There the current moves 140 million cubic metres of water per second, over 5000 times more than the mighty Amazon.

Sandwiched between an outer ring of westerly winds to the north and an inner ring of easterly winds to the south, lies a region of intense low pressures or depressions. If you look at any satellite map of the Antarctic, you will see an endless series of depressions. They scud round the edge of the ocean at a rate of 600–1000 kilometres a day. It is these depressions that produce the bad weather typical of the Southern Ocean.

In addition to its dreadful stormy nature, the Southern Ocean is also hazardous because of ice. Each winter, much of the Southern Ocean simply freezes over. At its peak 20 million kilometres of ice are produced, covering 57 percent of the ocean's total surface. This massive environmental change, by far the biggest in nature, dominates the natural cycle in the Antarctic. Nearly all the region's wildlife obtains its food from the sea and would starve without access to it. So, as the ice advances each winter, the wildlife is driven north, often way past the Polar Front. Most animals spend the winter months in the open sea, only returning south to breed when the summer brings a thaw and the ice retreats again.

On first impressions, the Southern Ocean appears to be full of life. As our boat sailed south of the Polar Front, there were almost always birds riding the waves with us, the albatrosses, in particular, seeming as loyal as the Ancient Mariner described. Occasionally, we would sail into a swarm of krill stretching for kilometres, a pink sea of tiny crustaceans. On reaching one of the isolated islands, we were overwhelmed by the millions of penguins, seabirds and seals that breed there in the summer. But these scenes of plenty are misleading. Antarctic wildlife tends to occur in crowds and away from the 'hot spots' the ocean is almost empty of life. If all the Antarctic's penguins were spread throughout the Southern Ocean, there would be just 0.12 milligram of penguin per square metre.

A black-browed albatross searches the Southern Ocean for food – one of four albatross species that breeds south of the Polar Front.

THE APPROXIMATE POSITION OF THE ANTARCTIC POLAR FRONT

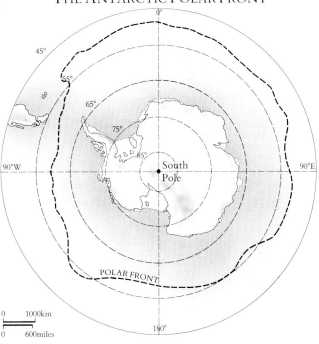

The patchy nature of Antarctic wildlife is due to the distribution of the tiny plants called phytoplankton that live in the surface waters. The phytoplankton start the ocean food chain, trapping the sun's energy through photosynthesis. The low temperature of Antarctic waters might be expected to slow down phytoplankton growth but the Southern Ocean makes up for the cold by being very rich in nutrients. The vertical movement of water at the Polar Front and the widespread turbulence of the ocean combine to bring a constant supply of vital minerals to the plankton. In particular, the Southern Ocean has high levels of two key nutrients, phosphates and nitrates, often several times higher than in other oceans. This and the continuous 24 hour daylight of the summer months provide the perfect conditions for phytoplankton blooms to flourish. In places, huge areas of the ocean turn green as the plankton rush to photosynthesize before winter steals away the sun. But the turbulence that brings up the minerals also ensures that these green patches are widely separated and very unpredictable.

The next step up the food chain ladder is occupied by the animal plankton, or zooplankton. They come in an enormous variety of shapes and sizes but by far the most important are the shrimp-like crustaceans called krill. Just 5 centimetres long, krill can occur in swarms so dense and so large that they turn the surface of the ocean red for kilometres. Like birds in a flock, the several thousands of individuals per square metre in a krill swarm show amazing co-ordination, swimming parallel to each other and altering course together. The total number of krill in the Southern Ocean is estimated to be a staggering 600 million million, making krill easily the most numerous creature on Earth. Based on this estimate, their total weight is 650 million tonnes, far greater than that of the world's human population.

The krill is the cornerstone of the Antarctic's ecology. Whales, seals, penguins and many other seabirds depend on it for their basic food. In the first half of this century, it is thought that whales alone were taking 150 million tonnes of krill a year. In comparison, our annual world fish catch weighs 70 million tonnes. Since then, people have vastly reduced whale populations, which has left far more krill for other creatures. The massive increase in fur seal numbers and the steady climb in penguin populations in the last 20 years reflect the bounty now available. People have also tried to exploit the krill directly, using sonar to detect the swarms. During the 1979–80 season, krill fishing reached a peak with half a million tonnes caught, but it soon declined. Krill goes rotten quickly after it is caught and it proved difficult to arouse consumer interest. For the wildlife of Antarctica, it is good news that our taste does not run to krill.

The best device for catching krill has to be the baleen plates of the baleen whales. These slender plates of horny keratin hang in two rows from the roof of the whale's mouth. They act as filters, straining sea water to separate off the plankton. Seven of the 11 species of baleen whales come south to feed in the Southern Ocean for the summer and all search for zooplankton and, in particular, krill. The giant among them is the blue whale which reaches a maximum length of about 30 metres and a weight of 150–200 tonnes. It is the largest animal on Earth and would have outclassed even the greatest of the dinosaurs, yet it feeds almost exclusively on tiny krill. There are thought to be just 1000 blue whales left of a pre-whaling population of 200 000. More mysterious is the 22–24 metre-long pygmy blue whale. This close relative of the blue whale has only recently been recognized and very little is known about its lifestyle.

The next largest whale to visit the Southern Ocean is the fin whale, which grows up to 20–23 metres and weighs 45–75 tonnes. It is the fastest of the large whales and the commonest, with an estimated southern hemisphere population of 85 000–100 000. Slightly smaller is the sei whale, which measures 15–18 metres although it weighs in at only to 20–25 tonnes. Sei whales rarely go further south than 55 degrees and keep well clear of any ice.

The southern right whale was so named by whalers because it was the 'right' whale to catch, being slow swimming and floating when dead. At 13.5–17 metres long and weighing 40–80 tonnes, it yielded large quantities of valuable oil. Unlike the larger baleen whales, the right whale does not have a streamlined torpedo shape. Its massive head takes up a quarter of its body length and is covered with callosities. These crusty skin growths are homes for thriving colonies of barnacles, parasitic worms and whale lice. The skin of the humpback whale is also encrusted with barnacles. This 13–18 metre long whale, weighing 25–30 tonnes, gets its name from its humped profile when diving. It has extremely long flippers which are up to a third of its body length. The humpback tends to stay near the coast and so was easy prey when whaling began in the Southern Ocean. By the 1960s, stocks had been reduced to below 3000 from a pre-whaling population estimated at 100 000, but now they seem to be increasing. The smallest baleen whale to venture south is the minke. Measuring just 8 metres long and 8–12 tonnes in weight, the minke largely escaped the attention of the whalers and still survives in considerable numbers. Ironically, it is the only baleen whale that can still be taken legally in Antarctic waters.

The sight of baleen whales hoovering up the krill is very impressive, as we discovered during 10 days spent watching humpbacks feeding along the Antarctic Peninsula. Like the whales, we took advantage of the 24 hours of daylight in January

and watched them practically non-stop. As the ice retreats, the whales come down from warmer northern waters where they have spent the Antarctic winter. All along the Peninsula they search the sheltered bays for swarms of krill. It is often calm and peaceful in the bays but, when we were sitting in a tiny rubber dinghy one evening, the mill pond was disrupted only by 15 pairs of whales breaking the surface to breathe or feed.

The humpbacks were using two different methods of feeding depending, it seemed, on the depth and density of the krill. If a swarm was centred near the surface, the whales would lunge up from below. For a few exciting seconds the ocean would appear to fry as thousands of tiny krill attempted to escape. Then, with a great rush of sound, the whales would break the surface with vast mouths agape and swallow a mouthful of krill soup. Usually two whales worked together in this lunge feeding but, once, we watched three whales working in a perfectly co-ordinated line of mouths.

When the krill were at greater depths and more widely spread, two humpbacks working together would dive simultaneously. For a few moments all would be quiet and then, mysteriously, bubbles would appear on the surface. From the crow's-nest of our ship it was obvious that these bubbles were forming the edges of a circle. Suddenly, just as the two half circles of bubbles met to complete the trap, the two whales would thunder up through the centre of the circle with mouths open. In this bubble-netting method, two whales gradually release great columns of bubbles, creating a net to concentrate the krill. They then swim straight through the centre of their trap and feast on the enriched krill soup. What impressed me most was that to create the edges of the bubble net, the whales had to spiral round each other as they dived and returned to the surface. It was a beautiful underwater ballet played out by two 30 tonne creatures.

All the baleen whales have slightly different ways of catching their plankton. The southern right whale swims open-mouthed along the surface, skimming for its prey. The sei whale either skims like the southern right or swallows like the minke, blue, fin and humpback. A swallower takes in a mouthful of sea water and some krill by sweeping through the water with its jaws wide open, its tongue inverted and the grooves beneath its chin and throat expanded. It then snaps the jaws shut, everts the tongue and contracts the grooves to force most of the water out through the baleen plates. This leaves a thick krill soup to be swallowed.

Once baleen whales have found a source of krill, their feeding never seems to stop. Each day in summer they catch 3–4 percent of their own body weight in krill. For a 150–tonne blue whale, that means up to 6 tonnes, or 6 million individual krill a day. To avoid competition, the different whales have different types of baleen plates.

TOP LEFT A fur seal plays among the kelp round the island of South Georgia.
BELOW LEFT Krill is the basis of the Antarctic food chain.

The right whales have the finest of all and trap the smallest prey, tiny copepods forming a major part of their diet. The blue whale has far larger, coarser baleens and sieves out only the larger adult krill. The different whales also favour different parts of the Southern Ocean.

As winter approaches the krill disperse, most of them to graze beneath the increasing pack ice, and all the baleen whales except the minke head north. The six months they have spent feeding in Antarctic waters have built up their blubber and fat-reserves for breeding. They will draw on these during the winter for none of the baleen whales feed much in the north. The lean period puts a great strain on them, particularly the breeding females. A newborn blue whale calf gains 80 kilograms every day while suckling at its mother's breast. To meet her baby's needs, the mother must produce 130 kilograms of milk per day. Not surprisingly, when summer comes and the whales return to the Antarctic, their blubber is thin and their condition poor.

Though they still remain very mysterious creatures, squid also play a very major role in the Southern Ocean's ecology. Squid belong to the same group of animals – the molluscs – as snails, whelks and cockles. Within that group, their particular family is called the cephalopods and includes squid, octopuses and cuttlefish as well as squid. All the cephalopods live in the sea but, unlike other marine molluscs, they are not tied to the seabed. They developed buoyant chambers in their shells and so can be free swimming. The cephalopods are highly active, voracious carnivores, able to move rapidly around the sea using their unique form of locomotion, jet propulsion. To catch their prey they have an unusual and impressive armoury of weapons.

Squid are the only cephalopods found in significant numbers in the Antarctic. They are equipped with 10 muscular tentacles, each with rows of hundreds of powerful suckers. Round the edge of each sucker is a sharp ring that can easily cut a circle through human skin. At the centre of the tentacles are very powerful jaws called a beak because they resemble the sharp beak of a parrot. Any prey caught in the grasping tangle of tentacles is quickly drawn into the slicing beak.

There are thought to be about 20 species of squid in the Southern Ocean but little is known about them. This is particularly true of the many species that live at great depths. Others spend the day in deeper water, and migrate to the surface at night in large, protective shoals. They come to shallow water to feed and to perform extravagant courtship displays. The majority of the deep-sea species are covered in tiny organs that produce light. Perhaps, in the inky depths of the Southern Ocean, these lights are used for communication. They could help to keep shoals together, attract mates or lure prey. Squid living in shallower water, where daylight penetrates, have luminous organs on

A sleeping humpback whale exhales.

their undersides. These may help them to avoid predators. By carefully regulating the light they produce to match down-welling daylight, the squid can break up or hide their silhouette from a predator below.

Squid need such protection because they are important sources of food for many of the Antarctic's larger animals. Sperm whales eat virtually nothing except squid and one was found with the remains of over 18 000 squid in its stomach. By deep diving these whales can get at the larger squid that live at great depths. Smaller squid species which live in shallower water are an important food source for other Antarctic wildlife including seals, albatrosses and penguins. Squid are a particular favourite with emperor penguins. Grey-headed albatrosses take about 14 000 tonnes of squid annually and during their vital chick-rearing period, squid represent 50 percent of their food. Humans are also turning their attention to squid and large commercial squid fisheries are beginning to develop in the Southern Ocean.

The lack of knowledge about squid extends to their numbers. However, it has been estimated that 35 million tonnes of squid are taken each year in the Antarctic by seabirds, seals and whales. To support this annual loss, the population must be at least three times the size. So the estimate suggests that there are 100 million tonnes of squid, making them a massive part of the Southern Ocean's food chain. In comparison, fish seem to play a fairly small part in the Antarctic's ecosystem, providing only 15 million tonnes of food per year to birds and seals.

Of the 20 000 or so species of fish in the world, only 120 are found south of the Antarctic Polar Front. This is less than 1 percent of the total in an ocean that makes up 10 percent of the world's total area of ocean. The paucity of Antarctic fish is particularly noticeable when their numbers are compared with those in Arctic seas. Most of the world's commercial fisheries look to the Arctic for their catches. The massive shoals of herring, capelin and sandlance there provide the staple diet for birds, seals and whales. Shoals on this scale are practically unknown in the Antarctic.

The scarcity of fish in Antarctic waters cannot be due simply to the cold, harsh conditions because Arctic seas can be just as demanding. The main problem seems to be breeding. Spawning fish need shallow water where they can leave their fertilized eggs to develop on or near the seabed. In the Arctic, the continental shelf is near the surface, at the right depth to provide large areas of shallow water which make ideal spawning grounds. The Antarctic continental shelf, in contrast, is at great depth and offers very little suitable spawning habitat.

Although the Antarctic has relatively few fish, most of those that do occur are endemic, or found only in the Southern Ocean. In the shallower, coastal waters over

85 percent of the species are endemic, cut off from other oceans by deep surrounding seas and specially adapted for life in the world's coldest waters. Most of these endemics belong to just one order, the Nototheniiformes, and split into four families – the Antarctic cod (Nototheniidae), the plunder fish (Harpagiferidae), the dragon fish (Bathydraconidae) and the ice fish (Channichthyidae). They are generally small fish, few growing to more than 50 centimetres. Typically, they have spines along their backs and large, bony pectoral fins, which they spread out for support when resting on the seabed. Most nototheniiform species are bottom dwellers, though several have young that are pelagic, or live in the open ocean. Only one species, the Antarctic silverfish, is pelagic all year round.

Antarctic fish are fitted in many clever ways for life in the Southern Ocean, including breeding adaptations. While an Arctic cod will release over 6 million eggs, the nototheniiforms rarely lay more than a couple of thousand. Though smaller in number, their eggs are big and become larger further south, reaching up to 4.5 millimetres in diameter. The precious, yolk-rich eggs are carefully guarded in well-defended nests. The timing of egg-laying is crucial in the Antarctic. By spawning in early winter, the fish ensure that the fry hatch out at the beginning of summer just as the phytoplankton blooms are occurring. Once the eggs hatch, the adults continue to guard their young. Parental care is unusual among fish which, as a group, generally invest little time in their eggs or fry. But such care is very much the rule among animals living in extreme environments. In Antarctica, even animals as diverse as molluscs and crustaceans tend their young.

Another characteristic adaptation of Antarctic fish is a reduction in the number of red blood cells and the haemoglobin pigment they carry. Animals need oxygen to release energy from food and enable them to be active. Oxygen is not very soluble in blood so most animals that have blood rely on haemoglobin to transport oxygen round their body. The haemoglobin fixes oxygen from the lungs of air breathers or the gills of aquatic breathers and carries it to the parts of the body that need it.

Most Antarctic fish have half the haemoglobin count of fish living in temperate seas, while one group, the ice fish, have no haemoglobin at all. They are the only vertebrates on Earth that completely lack haemoglobin. There are about 15 species of Antarctic ice fish and most are active, predatory animals. They lack scales and have large spade-shaped heads with strong jaws armed with sharp teeth. Their colourless blood gives them an extraordinary appearance, leaving them ghostly white with large cream-coloured gills. If you have ever cut open a fish such as a mackerel, you will know that its gills are a deep bright red. The haemoglobin concentrates at the gills to pick up the

ABOVE *Flocks of cape petrels follow feeding humpbacks to exploit the krill the whales drive to the surface.*

RIGHT *Three humpback whales co-operate in lunge feeding for krill near the surface.*

BELOW *Krill-rich water is sieved through the baleen plates of a humpback whale.*

oxygen that is so important to an active fish like a mackerel. Yet ice fish manage to remain active without any haemoglobin at all.

Part of the answer to this puzzle lies in the Southern Ocean itself. Rough, well-stirred seas tend to be rich in oxygen and cold water can hold more oxygen than warm water. As a result there is a greater concentration of oxygen in the Southern Ocean than in most other oceans in the world. Another factor is that cold tends to slow an animal down, reducing its metabolic rate and so reducing the amount of energy it needs. The respiratory rates of all Antarctic fish are well below those of fish in temperate waters and ice fish have metabolic rates half those of their Antarctic neighbours. With such low energy demands and such high local oxygen supplies, ice fish have little need for haemoglobin. So they have saved the energy required to produce haemoglobin and developed other adaptations instead. The volume of blood in an ice fish is two or three times greater than that of other bony fish. Almost a tenth of its body weight is taken up with blood that transports oxygen. Its blood circulates faster because the ice fish has larger blood vessels and a heart that is up to three times as big and beats up to 10 times as fast as a similarly sized red-blooded fish. It has large gills to improve oxygen uptake and also takes oxygen in through its scaleless, highly vascularized skin. All these adaptations enable the ice fish to lead a surprisingly active life.

Antarctic fish have to cope with life in an ocean that is often very close to freezing and, in the winter, does actually freeze over. While fresh water freezes at zero degrees centigrade, sea water contains salts which lower its freezing temperature to minus 1.9 degrees centigrade. The blood and body tissues of fish contain lower concentrations of salts than the sea and so tend to freeze at minus 0.7 degrees centigrade. Even in the summer, the temperature in much of the Southern Ocean is around minus 1 degree centigrade. This is cold enough to freeze the tissues of most fish, resulting in certain death.

The majority of Antarctic fish have got around this problem by developing a form of antifreeze in their blood. The antifreeze consists of glycoproteins, a mixture of sugars and proteins. These interfere with the formation of ice crystals in the blood by interacting with the faces of the crystals and hindering the addition of further water molecules to the crystals. The antifreeze reduces the temperature at which a fish's blood freezes to as low as minus 2.75 degrees centigrade. The effect is very dramatic. In the middle of winter, when the top few metres of the ocean is solid ice, fish survive in the near frozen waters below. Shallow water species are particularly at risk. They can often be seen frozen to the seabed by a collar of ice, yet they survive.

Despite all these adaptations, fish play a relatively small part in the ecology of the Southern Ocean. In most oceans, fish are among the main consumers and an important prey for other animals higher in the food chain. In the Antarctic food chain, birds and mammals replace fish as the main consumers. Perhaps birds and mammals are better suited to the cold conditions because they are warm-blooded. They are also well insulated, can store substantial energy reserves and are able to travel enormous distances in search of food. These features are particularly important in the Southern Ocean where food supplies are patchy and unpredictable. Each summer, a short pulse of solar energy stimulates the phytoplankton blooms. These in turn fuel the krill, the most important primary consumer in the Antarctic food chain. Krill's tendency to form large, discrete swarms leaves its predators, the mammals and seabirds, searching for rich jackpots in an otherwise barren ocean.

The birds of the Antarctic are, in the main, adapted to an ocean-going life. Almost all the birds ultimately rely on the sea for their food and many are pelagic wanderers that only come to land to breed. Of the world's 310 or more species of seabirds, less than 50 are found south of the Polar Front. They comprise seven penguins; four albatrosses; twenty three typical petrels, prions and shearwaters; four storm petrels; two diving petrels; one gull; three terns; two skuas; two sheathbills and one cormorant. Though the number of species is small, the estimates of total populations are impressive. The four albatross species together total about 140 000 pairs. Penguins are thought to number 17–20 million breeding pairs. The petrels that nest in burrows are particularly difficult to count but one estimate is 150 million birds. The populations also look enormous when the birds are breeding, packed together on a tiny island. But outside the breeding season, when the birds are roaming over the 36 million square kilometres of the Southern Ocean, they are spread very thinly.

For years scientists have studied Antarctic seabirds on dry land when they settle to breed, but this is only a small part of their lives. Their wanderings at sea, which have long been something of a mystery, are now being revealed with the help of modern electronics. A radio transmitter no larger than a matchbox can be mounted harmlessly on an albatross's back. The transmitter sends regular signals to a satellite, disclosing the albatross's every move. We used daily satellite data to track the birds for almost six weeks as they searched the Southern Ocean for the elusive patches of krill. Most of the time only a handful of birds followed our boat but there always seemed to be an albatross.

The wandering albatross, with a 3.5 metre wingspan, is the largest seabird in the world. Like all the albatrosses, it hugs the waves with effortless ease, flying at great speed while never seeming to beat its wings at all. Satellite tracking has shown that the wandering albatross can reach an astonishing 88 kilometres per hour and keep going for days at a time at an average speed of over 30 kilometres per hour. The technique it uses to maintain this record-breaking flight is common to all the albatrosses. The bird first makes a shallow dive with its wings held in an 'M' to reduce drag and increase speed. As it nears the surface of the sea, it turns along the trough of a wave and straightens its wings for maximum lift. Then, using the up-current off the crest of the wave, it quickly gains height. When the albatross begins to lose speed, it simply starts the cycle again. In this way the albatross can achieve great speeds over enormous distances without beating its wings or expending too much energy. A wandering albatross can even circumnavigate the globe many times. But its method of flight does require wind and only the southern hemisphere, with its great unbroken expanses of ocean, seems to provide enough. Most albatrosses are restricted to the windiest latitudes of 40 and 50 degrees South. Further south than 56 degrees, the Antarctic Peninsula and the ice slows down the wind and makes life difficult for the albatrosses.

The albatrosses together with the petrels make up the majority of the Antarctic's seabirds. Both belong to an order of birds, the Procellariiformes, in which there is an enormous range of sizes. The wandering albatross is the largest member, weighing 7.7–9.5 kilograms. The smallest is the tiny Wilson's storm petrel which weighs just 30–40 grams. Though no larger than a house martin, the storm petrel seems completely at home in a massive sea, tiptoeing from one wave crest to another.

Birds in the order are characterized by tube-like nostrils on the top of the beak. The function of the tubular nostrils is not entirely clear. Most scientists think they are used to excrete excess salt which could be vital to birds living almost entirely at sea with no access to fresh water. Others have experimented to see if the nostrils give the birds a heightened sense of smell. This might enable them to sniff out their particular burrow when returning to the nesting colony or to locate food to scavenge on the surface of the ocean. However, most birds have a very poor sense of smell, and the petrels and albatrosses are unlikely to be any different.

After spending many hours at sea, with just the occasional albatross for company, we finally saw in the distance the krill swarm that we and the birds had been searching for. White specks circled against a bright blue sky and, below, black spots could be glimpsed between the rolling waves. As our boat drew closer, the white dots became wheeling birds and the black dots, penguins. The surface of the sea seemed to boil as over a thousand birds fed excitedly on the krill hiding below. Penguins kept popping up after completing dives, while petrels scooped krill near the surface and albatrosses performed inelegant duck-dives. Up to 10 different species of birds were involved in the frantic search for food. The most fascinating thing about watching these feeding

RIGHT Albatrosses follow a hunting killer whale, hoping for something to scavenge.

BELOW Giant petrels rip into an elephant seal carcass. Cape petrels wait for scraps.

flocks is that, as with the baleen whales, the different species use different techniques to catch krill.

The flightless penguins have the advantage that they can dive down to get their prey. Where we were, in the north near the Antarctic Polar Front, the two common penguins feeding on krill are the macaroni and gentoo. The macaroni gets its name from a characteristic tuft of yellow feathers on either side of its black head. The slightly larger gentoo penguin has an obvious white patch above its eye. Both tend to fish in flocks and, when you dive with them, you are rewarded with a spectacular underwater display. Tens of penguins suddenly leave the surface together and, with an elegance they possess only under water, fly down to the blue depths below. Both species can dive down to 100 metres or so and have swimming speeds of 1.9 metres per second. With such a similar feeding technique, the two penguin species could be in close competition for krill. They avoid this by having hunting grounds that rarely overlap. Gentoos tend to be inshore feeders, going only about 30 kilometres from their nest sites. Macaronis are offshore feeders and venture as far as 115 kilometres to find krill, a remarkable achievement for birds that cannot fly.

The flying birds in the feeding flocks are restricted largely to the surface. Our divers saw small balls of krill being driven up near the surface by penguins. Black-browed albatrosses dived down a metre or so to grab at this prey. The two species of diving petrel also took krill below the surface. Their short powerful wings can propel these small birds to 10 metres down in the water. If the krill come to the surface, many other petrels can feast on the bounty. The prions use a particularly ingenious method. A prion's bill is fringed with lamellae which, like those in a flamingo's beak, act as a filter. Dove prions strain crustaceans from the sea while seeming to hydroplane along the surface, with wings outstretched and bill submerged, using their feet to drive them forward. Like the penguins, the different species of prions tend to go for different prey, those with smaller beaks and thinner lamellae catching smaller zooplankton. One was found to have 41 000 individual prey items in its stomach. The storm petrels flutter over the surface, picking up the scraps that others leave behind. From a distance they look like beautiful black butterflies dancing on the waves. Their legs are very long for such tiny birds and their feet keep bouncing off the water surface. Like Saint Peter, they seem to be walking on water and so their family became known as Saint Peter's birds or petrels.

Occasionally the feeding flocks were joined by spectacularly mobile fur seals, long whiskers trailing from their noses and large fore-flippers propelling them at great speed. They twisted and turned among the massive ball of plankton while the krill parted in waves, trying to escape the seals' hungry bite. Under water, the Antarctic fur seals are the greatest acrobats of the Southern Ocean. The group of seals to which they belong includes the sea lions and all the members have external ears, and look and behave very much like sea lions. Antarctic fur seals get their name from their thick coats, which made them much sought after by commercial sealers and nearly led to their extinction in the nineteenth century.

Six species of seal inhabit the Antarctic, each specially adapted for life in a particular part of the Southern Ocean. The toughest of them all, the Weddell seal, survives among the fast ice of the deep south, feeding on squid and, particularly, fish. A little further north, the Ross and crabeater seals live among the pack ice. Ross seals are very rarely seen and no one knows exactly how many of them there are. They are thought to feed mainly on squid. Less elusive are the crabeaters which number 14–30 million, making them the commonest large mammals on Earth after humans. Despite their name, crabeater seals eat krill. Usually a little further north, but moving with the ice, are the leopard seals. While half their diet is krill, the leopard seals can become among the most impressive predators in the ocean, taking a wide variety of prey. The two northernmost seals are the fur and the elephant seal. Elephant seals are the largest of all the seals, with males reaching 4 tonnes, and feed mainly on fish and squid.

Fur seals are important predators of krill and, like penguins, can easily dive to 100 metres. A typical foraging trip will take a group of fur seals 60–90 kilometres from the shore and they must catch thousands of krill each per trip. To keep up speed on the way to the krill swarms, the seals often porpoise through the water. They make a beautiful sight as they break the surface, still wet and shiny, and perform a curving leap. Air offers far less resistance to their motion than water and so the more time they spend porpoising, the faster they travel. Using radio transmitters, the movements of fur seals can now be monitored round the clock. Seven seals were recorded making more than 4000 dives during 36 days at sea. Three-quarters of these dives were performed at night with peak activity at dawn and dusk. The nighttime dives were much shallower than the daytime ones. Each night, the massive krill swarms tend to migrate up towards the surface and clearly the seals have learnt to exploit the daily rhythm of krill movements.

The groups of birds and seals feeding at sea do not prey solely on krill. Studies in the Scotia Sea, the southern extension of the Atlantic Ocean, suggest that seals and birds between them consume 23 million tonnes of food a year. Of that 70 percent is krill, 16 percent is squid and 8 percent, fish. But there are other predators in the Southern Ocean that concentrate much more on animals higher in the food chain. These are the toothed whales, or odontocetes, a group that includes the dolphins.

Apart from seals, the baleen and toothed whales are the only mammals indigenous to the Antarctic. The majority of the toothed whales are far smaller than most of the baleen whales. As a result, few of the toothed whales were ever hunted and many remain mysterious, rarely seen animals. The hourglass dolphin, measuring 1.5–2 metres long, is the only small dolphin found in the south. It is beautifully patterned with a black and white hourglass design. Larger are Arnoux's beaked whale, up to 9.75 metres long, and the southern bottlenosed whale, reaching 7.5 metres long. These whales, which are almost impossible to tell apart at sea, range as far south as the ice edge. They both dive for their food, preying almost exclusively on deep-water squid.

The largest toothed whale that ventures south to the Antarctic is the sperm whale. The females and young stay in warmer seas but the adult male sperm whales, which are about 15 metres long and weigh around 45 tonnes, come to the Southern Ocean in search of squid. They are superlative divers, going as deep as 1000 metres to discover enormous squid with tentacles up to 9 metres long. No one has ever seen the tussle that goes on at great depths between these giants. However, the heads of many sperm whales are covered in scars left by squid suckers, so clearly squid are no easy prey.

A sperm whale has an enormous snout which takes up about a quarter of its length and accounts for a third of its total weight. The snout contains a clear liquid wax called spermaceti oil, which allows the whale to regulate its buoyancy and plays a vital part in its remarkable diving abilities. Spermaceti oil was highly prized by the whaling industry as a lubricant and detergent. For the whale, it is a minutely variable source of ballast and takes a great deal of the effort out of deep diving. The whale's snout is richly supplied with blood capillaries which can cool or warm the oil. The whale can also bring the oil's temperature down by drawing cold water through the blowhole into the nasal passage. As the spermaceti cools, it contracts and becomes denser, pulling the whale's head down into a diving position. To ascend, the whale simply redirects the flow of blood so that it warms the spermaceti oil and reduces its density. With its trim readjusted, the sperm whale makes an easy passage back to the surface.

More famous and with a frighteningly catholic taste in prey are the killer whales, which are widely spread throughout the Southern Ocean. They are the only whales that take warm-blooded mammals and, in the Antarctic, their main prey are other whales and seals. Killers hunt together in groups called pods. Members of a pod coordinate their movements through an endless stream of clicks and calls. They are the fastest of the whales, easily maintaining a speed of 25 knots, and form a menacing sight as their long black dorsal fins slice through the ocean. Killer whales penetrate deep into

A humpback whale travels south along the Antarctic Peninsula.

the pack ice and are quick to follow the giant icebreakers as they cut a way through the ice at the beginning of summer. Stories abound of hungry whales smashing up through thinner ice to grab unsuspecting prey. A member of Scott's expedition even described his desperate rush for thicker ice while being pursued by killer whales.

Their threat to humans is probably overstated but killer whales are certainly major predators of seals. The commonest seals in the Antarctic, the crabeaters, completely avoid land. They spend their entire time either in the water or on blocks of ice and so are always exposed to killer whales. Observations of their capture are rare but one group of scientists witnessed an extraordinary event. The scientists were based for months at the Argentine station on the Melchior Islands, just off the Antarctic Peninsula. The currents there are strong and large pieces of ice carrying seal passengers regularly drifted by the station. In the middle of an icefloe the seals were usually safe from attack but the local pod of killer whales had developed an ingenious technique. Swimming together along an icefloe, the whales would suddenly make a co-ordinated leap from the water. Their combined return to the ocean created a wave large enough to wash the seals from their icy retreat. Once in the water, the seals were easy pickings for the whales.

The killers also tackle much larger prey. While searching for krill swarms, we came across the remains of what had clearly been a young baleen whale. As we approached, the threatening black dorsal fins of departing killers were still visible on the horizon. Yet already a squabble of hungry birds surrounded the remains of the whale's distinctive ribbed throat floating on the surface. Scavenging is an important option for some seabirds. Most of these scavengers were giant petrels which seem to be the main 'vultures' of the Southern Ocean. Large, noisy birds, they use their powerful hooked beak to rip open carcasses and see off any rivals for the prize. Tiny Wilson's storm petrels fluttered over the scrum, stealing minute scraps of flesh and oil. These smallest petrels were dwarfed by the largest in their group, the wandering albatrosses, which also fought to get their share.

The wandering albatross is perhaps the most remarkable of all Antarctic birds. During the winter, when the sea ice reaches its greatest extent, the Southern Ocean is a dark and lonely place. In the south it is permanently dark and even in the far north, near the Polar Front, the days are short. The phytoplankton blooms have passed away and the massive swarms of krill have dispersed, some to die and others to winter beneath the sea ice. With the krill hidden from view, most of the birds have headed north into more temperate seas. The wandering albatross is among the few that remain. It has no choice: it has a chick to feed.

A wandering albatross chick endures the worst of the winter blizzards

All through the winter, adult wandering albatrosses visit their nest every few days to feed their chick. Covered in thick woolly down and insulated by a layer of fat, the chick waits on the nest, often up to its neck in driven snow. Its parents would have had difficulty finding a suitable nest site. Albatrosses are masters of the air but find it very difficult to take off from land. They need a cliff to launch off and strong winds to carry them away. So they must nest on islands and those islands must be accessible year round. Just south of the Antarctic Polar Front there are a handful of islands that meet their requirements. Among the loneliest places on Earth, these islands on the edge are precious breeding grounds for much of the Antarctic's wildlife.

FOLLOWING PAGE An adult wandering albatross tests
the wind before returning to sea after feeding its chick.

CHAPTER THREE

ISLANDS
ON THE
EDGE

BOUVETØYA IS THE most inaccessible place on Earth. This tiny windswept island in the Southern Ocean covers an area of only 50 square kilometres. Almost entirely covered in ice, it will go years without receiving a visitor. Even finding it in an atlas is extremely difficult. The edge of the map of the Antarctic seems to show just the endless blue of open ocean. But if you look very carefully, you may find a tiny dot for Bouvetøya, to the south between the Cape of South Africa and South America. You may also see a handful of other islands lost in the expanse of ocean that leaves Antarctica so isolated. Heard Island, to the south-east of Australia, is a glacier in the ocean, almost permanently covered in mist. The islands in the South Sandwich chain are all active volcanoes that pierce straight out of the world's roughest sea. Even the largest island, South Georgia, is only about 170 kilometres long and 2–30 kilometres wide. These islands on the edge seem almost too small to matter, but to many of the Antarctic's animals they are of great importance.

Within the Antarctic Polar Front there are three types of island. Right by the continent itself lie the Antarctic coastal islands, which are almost permanently trapped by pack ice. They are directly influenced by the cold, dry air from the continent and have very similar weather. In summer, temperatures can rise to just above freezing but mean winter temperatures are minus 15–20 degrees centigrade or lower. It never rains on these islands, it only snows. Ice-free rock is rare and the only plants are lichens. Further north and sprinkled all round the continent are the maritime Antarctic islands.

The Three Brothers tower over the Neumayer Glacier, South Georgia.

THE ANTARCTIC CONTINENT AND ITS SURROUNDING ISLANDS

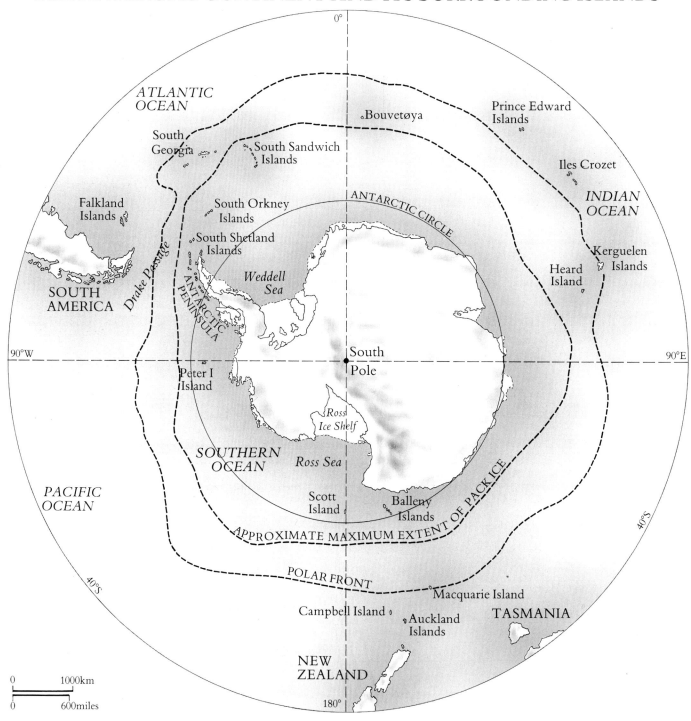

0°

ATLANTIC
OCEAN

Bouvetøya

Prince Edward
Islands

South
Georgia

South Sandwich
Islands

Iles Crozet

INDIAN
OCEAN

Falkland
Islands

South Orkney
Islands

ANTARCTIC CIRCLE

South Shetland
Islands

Kerguelen
Islands

SOUTH
AMERICA

Drake Passage

ANTARCTIC PENINSULA

Weddell
Sea

Heard
Island

90°W

90°E

Peter I
Island

South
Pole

Ross
Ice Shelf

SOUTHERN
OCEAN

Ross Sea

PACIFIC
OCEAN

APPROXIMATE MAXIMUM EXTENT OF PACK ICE

Scott
Island

Balleny
Islands

40°S

POLAR FRONT

40°S

Macquarie Island

Campbell Island

Auckland
Islands

TASMANIA

NEW
ZEALAND

0   1000km

0   600miles

180°

They are only surrounded by sea ice in the winter and their weather is influenced by the Southern Ocean. Mean temperatures range from minus 7 degrees centigrade in winter to around freezing in summer, and there are often large ice-free areas. Although only two tiny flowering plants are able to exist on the maritime islands, slow-growing mosses form deep banks of peat. Further north still, scattered along the Polar Front, are just a handful of sub-Antarctic island groups. They rarely, if ever, get trapped in sea ice and are wet and windy, with climates dominated by the ocean that surrounds them. At sea level, winter temperatures often fall to just below freezing, while mean summer temperatures vary between freezing point and plus 3 degrees centigrade. The vegetation is far more extensive than on the inner islands, including large areas of tussock grass and several other flowering plants. However, no trees or shrubs survive the winter cold.

These islands are important to many Antarctic animals because they provide the only places for them to breed. Although the emperor penguin can lay its eggs on ice, all the other birds need bare rock and this is in very short supply anywhere other than the islands. Antarctica is only 2 percent ice free and just 13 species of flying birds find space there to nest. The vast majority of Antarctic birds depend on the islands. Even on these, suitable space is at such a premium that most birds breed in enormous colonies. Of the total world population of 6.5 million chinstrap penguins, 5 million nest on the South Sandwich Islands. It is very difficult to land on these bare volcanic peaks which rear up in the ocean kilometres from any other land. But a ship bobbing in the surf can give a view of one of nature's greatest spectacles. On Zavodovski Island, where more than 2 million penguins are believed to nest, white dots against the black volcanic ground seem to go on for ever, covering every centimetre of ground and disappearing up the sides of the mountain until they are lost in mist. Throughout the islands, wherever there are suitable sites, birds and seals breed in the thousands.

Since most Antarctic animals get their food from the sea, they must have access to the ocean when they breed. The annual advance and retreat of sea ice is the key factor that determines access for the wildlife. The coastal islands nearest to the continent are rarely released from the grip of sea ice. The maritime islands are not available to most birds and all seals until the summer, when the ice has retreated. Only the sub-Antarctic islands have this vital access year round. It is these islands on the edge that attract some of the most striking congregations of animals.

Everyone who has ever visited the largest of the sub-Antarctic islands, South Georgia, considers it a very special place. Like all the islands on the edge it is extremely remote. Port Stanley in the Falkland Islands is 1450 kilometres to the east, Antarctica is a similar distance to the south, while South Africa is 4800 kilometres away. The only

FOLLOWING PAGE Damien II *at anchor beside the British Antarctic Survey base, Bird Island.*

way to get to South Georgia is by ship and most people make the journey from Port Stanley. Travelling over some of the roughest waters in the world, it can take a very uncomfortable week. Then through the mist appear the most beautiful snow-capped peaks, which look almost as though someone had taken the Alps and dropped them straight into the ocean. Massive glaciers wind down between the mountains, constantly calving icebergs into the sea. All along the coast, fiords cut deep into the island and often steep cliffs rise straight out of the crashing waves. There is also a special ingredient rarely seen in the Antarctic – the colour green. In a region of ice and just a little rock, South Georgia seems a jungle. The land at sea level is covered with mosses, lichens and huge areas of towering tussock grass.

While South Georgia's scenery is impressive, its wildlife is even more so. As soon as we started to get close to the island, fur seals appeared from nowhere and porpoised beside the ship. The lone albatross that seemed to have been following us all the way from the Falklands was joined by many others. Finally, as the dark shapes of land started to appear on the horizon, the air literally filled with seabirds. We were approaching Bird Island, one of a number of small islands scattered round South Georgia. When Captain James Cook was circumnavigating Antarctica in 1775, it was Bird Island that he discovered first, nestling close to South Georgia's western tip. He had never seen so many birds and the name he gave the island remains apt. In the summer, virtually all of its 150 hectares are covered with breeding birds. More than 2500 pairs of wandering albatrosses nest among the tussock grass and up to 200 000 macaroni penguins fill the rocky hillsides with noisy squabbling. Even at night the air is full of beating wings as vast numbers of petrels use the cloak of dark to return to their burrows. All along South Georgia's coastline there are similar crowds of birds and seals.

South Georgia's climate is typical of the sub-Antarctic islands, being cold, wet and very, very windy. The island is, in fact, no closer to the South Pole than much of northern Europe is to the North Pole. However, South Georgia does not enjoy the warming influence of the Gulf Stream and the Antarctic continent is a far greater force for cold than the Arctic. As a result more than half of the island is covered by glaciers. Its average temperature is 2 degrees centigrade, which is very mild by Antarctic standards and in summer there are days of shirtsleeve weather. But in winter, massive storms thrash the coast, temperatures may drop to below minus 15 degrees centigrade and coastal snow may reach 2 metres deep. While the island hums with life in the summer, it is a very quiet and lonely place during the long Antarctic winter.

Most Antarctic animals cram their breeding season into the short summer months. Near continuous daylight provides the energy for the phytoplankton blooms

A male wandering albatross waits on his nest for his mate to return.

that kick-start the food chain. With lots to eat and plenty of time to find it, most parents can raise their young before the terrible winter bites. But the wandering albatross is such a big bird that its chicks cannot grow to full size within the summer months. So it has to include the winter in its breeding cycle.

The wandering albatross chick reaches its maximum size of 12 kilograms after about 220 days on the nest. It is then heavier than its parents and about the same weight as an adult mute swan. It is only when you sit beside a young wandering albatross that you really appreciate how big these chicks are. Sitting bolt upright on its simple nest, its beak is well above your head. Its size makes the chick fearless of predators and it happily tolerates a strange human alongside. But a gentle attempt to stroke its breast elicits a quick and painful snap from the enormous beak.

It takes wanderers just over 12 months to raise their chicks so the adults can only breed once every two years. In November, just as the chicks are almost ready to leave their nests, a new breeding cycle begins. These albatrosses live for over 80 years and tend to stick with one breeding partner for life. Since breeding last the partners have been apart, spending their lives alone at sea and now, somehow, find their way back to tiny Bird Island. The male wanderer is the first to arrive at the breeding site, preceding his mate by two weeks. The nests are traditional and a male usually returns to the same nest or one very close. Each year new mud is added to form what looks like a large upturned saucepan. A shallow depression in the top keeps the egg in place.

Once he has settled at the nest, the male waits patiently. He has probably not seen his mate for over a year and is keen to be there when she arrives. Suddenly she appears from nowhere, circling the island looking for her mate. Bird Island becomes a little like an international airport as the massive wanderers, like jumbo jets, prepare to land. Perfectly adapted for endless flight at sea, these birds do not find coming down to earth an easy task. After many preliminary circles, she drops her legs and spreads her feet. These air brakes slow her down but her landing is far from elegant. After tumbling through the tussock, she shakes her head high and cautiously approaches her mate.

Established pairs do not need much courtship and copulation is quick. The single white egg weighs a mighty 450 grams and is incubated for about 78 days. Both parents have to share this task, taking three to ten day shifts sitting on the nest. When the chick finally hatches it weighs just 350 grams. Both parents brood and feed it for about another seven weeks by which time the chick has grown tenfold and weighs 3 kilograms. Finally, when winter is in full swing, the adults leave the chick to return to the ocean and the full-time search for food. For the next four months the chick sits out

PREVIOUS PAGE A male wandering albatross displays to his mate, watched by another female.
RIGHT A copulating male wandering albatross on top of his mate.

some of the world's worst weather, often almost submerged in snow. Usually one of the parents comes with food every three days or so but sometimes dreadful storms at sea delay its return for weeks. The chick's survival depends entirely on how successful the adults are at scavenging the ocean. Wanderers tracked by satellite have gone all the way from South Georgia to the southern coast of Brazil in search of food. One female travelled over 13 951 kilometres in just under 17 days. In that time, she returned to the nest only twice to feed her chick.

Eventually spring comes round again and after nearly ten months on the nest the chick is getting ready to take its first flight. It has shed the coat of down that insulated it during the winter and for weeks it has been frantically exercising its wings in every gust of wind. The wanderers all nest by large cliffs where strong winds from the sea provide the updraughts they need and areas clear of tussock grass form runways where they can gather speed. Finally, around Christmas, the chick is ready to go. It runs towards the cliff, takes off on its first flight and in moments it has vanished, not to return to land again for years. Nobody is absolutely sure where the maturing albatrosses go but probably they circumnavigate the whole of Antarctica. Eventually, five to seven years later, they return to the same tiny islands where they were hatched but do not breed until they are seven to ten years old.

Wandering albatross chicks are not totally alone on South Georgia during the worst of the winter weather. King penguin chicks also sit out the storms in massive colonies. Adult kings are big birds, standing almost a metre tall and coming right up to one's waist. Like the wandering albatrosses, their great size means that their chicks are not able to reach full size in the short summer season. In fact, it takes king penguins a record 14–16 months to complete one breeding cycle. Over the winter months, the adults return to the sea to find food leaving the chicks on the beaches, huddled together for warmth and protection. These creches often contain thousands of penguin chicks and provide one of the Antarctic's most magnificent sights.

The king is the most familiar of the penguins, having been portrayed for years on the wrappers of chocolate biscuits. It is a very dignified, handsome bird, with a breast like a white shirt front and a flush of orange-yellow beneath the throat. The back and flippers are a shiny dark grey and behind each eye there is a bright patch of dark orange. The lower half of the bill also has a streak of brilliant orange. When it emerges fresh from the sea, glistening with water dripping from its flippers, there can hardly be a cleaner, smarter bird. The king is far bigger than most penguins and only the emperor penguin is larger. The emperor is only a little taller but almost twice as heavy, weighing up to 40 kilograms. It has more white behind the ears than the king and a pink rather

A wandering albatross regurgitates to its seven month old chick.

than orange streak on the lower half of the bill, but otherwise looks very similar. However, these birds can rarely be confused because their lifestyles are so different that their paths hardly ever cross. The emperor is the only bird in the world that can lay its eggs on ice and so it can breed on the very edge of Antarctica. The king needs to feed its chick throughout the winter and so must have year-round access to the sea. Only the islands on the northern edge, the sub-Antarctic islands, remain ice free all year and the king penguins are restricted to this area.

The king penguin does not make a nest. Instead, it incubates the single egg by holding it on the feet and covering it with a loose fold of overhanging skin. The adults are quite capable of waddling gently along with the egg in place. Because they incubate in this way, king penguins need to breed on flattish ground near the sea. The most suitable sites are the plains left by retreating glaciers. The snout of a glacier may be a kilometre or so back from the breaking waves, leaving a level field of grey moraine. Almost wherever these conditions exist, there is a king penguin colony. Sometimes just a few hundred birds breed together, but often there are thousands and thousands. The largest colony of all is that on Île aux Cochons in the Îles Crozet. At least 300 000 pairs nest side by side in a colony that stretches to the horizon. The colony doubled in size between 1966 and 1985, and numbers are still going up.

While walking through a king penguin colony, you are struck immediately by how tame the chicks are. Looking like fluffy brown bears, they quickly gather round as soon as you sit down. They spend their day together in loose creches of several thousand birds for protection against the elements and predators. Dotted among the sea of brown are the bright white breasts of the adults. Depending on the exact time of year, some adults are feeding chicks, others courting or moulting. There is a constant cacophony of calling birds and an all-pervading stench. In the larger colonies, the carpet of birds stretches on and on, filling the space between the mountains and the crashing sea.

The king penguin breeding cycle is complex and fascinating. Although it takes even longer than that of the wandering albatross, the king penguin manages to produce two chicks every three years. On South Georgia, the season begins in late October when newly moulted adults return to the colony, pair off, mate, and produce their single eggs. This first wave of breeders is made up of adults that for one reason or another failed to rear a chick during the previous season. They do not return to an empty colony. Throughout their courtship and incubation, they are surrounded by large chicks that have just survived their first winter. These juveniles have been tended by their parents since they hatched out the previous summer.

PREVIOUS PAGE King penguins emerge from the surf at St Andrew's Bay, South Georgia.
RIGHT A king penguin chick begs its parent for food.

By mid-January, the height of summer, the juveniles have fattened, moulted and left the colony for the ocean. The eggs laid by the first wave of breeders are starting to hatch and the young are fed by both parents on the abundant summer food. These new chicks grow rapidly and by mid-April, they weigh 10–12 kilograms and stand almost as tall as their parents. Meanwhile the parents of the now departed juveniles have laid again, forming a second wave of breeders. So by the end of April, as autumn storms become more frequent, the colony contains chicks at different stages in their development. Those of the first wave of breeders are already quite large and have a good chance of surviving the winter. Those of the second wave of breeders are much smaller and their chances of survival are correspondingly lower.

During the winter, storms cover the beaches in a carpet of snow and the chicks huddle together in one enormous creche for warmth. Their parents spend most of the winter at sea, returning only once every four or six weeks to give their chick a crop full of food. As the weather worsens and food becomes harder to find, the smaller chicks may die of hunger and exposure. By the end of the winter even the larger chicks have lost almost half their weight. When the summer comes round about 80 percent of the chicks have survived and the cycle starts all over again.

In three years a pair of king penguins will go through the different variations on this breeding pattern. If they lay early in the first year, their chick will be large by the autumn, survive the winter and leave the colony by January. The adults will then be second-wave breeders and have only a small chick by autumn of the second year. If that chick dies, they will be first-wave breeders in the third year. If the second-year chick survives the winter, it will not be large enough to go to sea until the very end of summer in the third year. The parents may lay again that year but the tiny chick is very unlikely to survive, and they will start the cycle again as first-wave breeders in spring of the fourth year. So in any three-year period, a pair of successful king penguins will rear two chicks.

Breeding success in king penguins is heavily dependent on the availability of food. Kings feed largely on small fish and cephalopods which they catch by pursuit diving. They display an agility under water unmatched by any other penguin, reaching speeds of over 12 kilometres per hour. Though most of the dives are less than 50 metres, king penguins can dive down to 290 metres. This is deeper than any other aquatic bird apart from the king's near relative, the emperor penguin. Studies round South Georgia have shown that kings will forage up to 250 kilometres away from their colonies. Towards the end of summer, a well-grown chick is being fed about every two to three days and receives 2–3 kilograms of squid on each visit. To catch this amount of food,

Displaying king penguins dotted amongst a creche of nearly full-grown chicks.

the adult has to expend about twice as much energy again. Each squid weighs 150–200 grams, so the parents have to catch between 50 and 90 squid each foraging trip. Since they make an average of 865 dives per trip, it appears that king penguins succeed in catching squid on fewer than 10 percent of their dives.

With so much going on at any one time, king penguin colonies are fascinating places to visit. One of the most extraordinary sights they offer is that of the adults taking a bath. Each morning, thousands of the birds resident in a colony waddle together down to the beach. Because it was once the snout of a glacier, the beach is long, flat and exposed. Huge waves rolling in from the south Atlantic smash on to the shingle and, at first, the birds appear wary of the water's power. But numbers gradually build up until there is enough shared confidence for all of them to rush into the pounding surf together. As they enter the medium in which they are most at home, the penguins' inelegant waddling changes to confident grace. Soon hundreds of kings are bobbing around together on the crests of the waves, totally unconcerned by the massive forces breaking beneath them. After 10 minutes of washing, the penguins make the altogether more dangerous return journey. Leaving the crest of a wave, they are often thrown against the beach as they struggle to escape nature's largest washing machine. Eventually, though, they emerge from the surf perfectly clean, dripping and glistening in the bright morning sun.

The king penguins have the surf to themselves through the winter, but from October their morning bath time is disturbed by tonnes of uninvited blubber. These are southern elephant seals, among the first animals to return at the start of spring. Most of their lives are spent at sea but they have to return to land to breed and give birth. The males return first, pulling their blubbery bulks up on to their traditional breeding beaches. These massive creatures reach over 5 metres long and weigh up to 4 tonnes. A month or so later, they are joined by the females, which are only about a third of their length and weight. Then the lonely strands of shingle, which were so quiet all winter, come alive with a spectacle of sex and violence that would have impressed the Romans.

Over half the world's 600 000 southern elephant seals return to South Georgia to breed. One beach alone, at the mouth of St Andrew's Bay, attracts over 6000 seals. The snout of a mighty glacier once filled the mouth but now the ice has retreated, leaving a flat black beach of fine glacial moraine. At either end of the beach, small hills offer a view of a solid line of elephant seals, which stretches for over 3 kilometres and is usually 10 to 20 animals thick. There is constant noise and action as females squabble, pups yelp for attention, and males roar and rear up in spectacular fights.

Only 30 percent of the males that haul up on the breeding beaches actually manage to copulate because the most high-ranking males claim and guard the vast majority of females. Unlike many other male seals, male elephant seals do not defend territories. Instead, the high-ranking males keep females in cohesive groups, or harems. The most successful may secure a harem of over 100 females. The key to success seems to be size, the biggest males tending to be the highest-ranking. They win more fights and their greater bulk allows them to sustain more easily the eight weeks of fasting they must endure while breeding on land. Their sole aim during this time is to mate with all the members of their harem and to achieve this they must be prepared to fight with many rival males. Smaller, lower-ranking males surround the harems or lie in the surf, waiting to sneak a moment for copulation.

A challenge from a rival generally starts with roaring. A male releases a long deep belching roar by blowing up the proboscis that gives these seals their name and lifting up its massive body. All day and through the night the roars echo round the bay. Roaring alone may sort out a dispute, the exact tone or strength of a male's roar seeming to indicate his size. As the season progresses, the seals start to recognize individual roars and remember fights they have lost or won. Gradually a clearer ranking order develops so that a single roar from a higher-ranking male will usually put off a challenger.

Sometimes, however, a fight does break out. Then two enormous males edge closer and closer until they are face to face. Their ceaseless roaring fills the beach as they slowly force up their enormous bulks into the air. Resting on their tails alone, they threaten each other with their full weights. Suddenly, with frightening force, they smash together and each seal tries to bite the other, ripping into the thick blubber of the neck. Usually the fights last just a minute or so but sometimes they continue for as long as a quarter of an hour. Time after time the giants clash until finally one retreats. The victor roars as his rival scampers with surprising speed through the harem, scattering females and crushing pups under his moving, rippling blubber. Both victor and loser are left exhausted and may be badly battered. By the end of the season, all the males are covered in scars and some have half their proboscis ripped away or chunks of loose flesh hanging from their bodies to remind them of past struggles.

As soon as they arrive at the breeding beaches, the females give birth to the single pups they conceived the previous year. Just 18 or 19 days after the birth, a female comes on heat, or into oestrus. The high-ranking males seem to be most experienced at recognizing this crucial time. They are thought to do so mainly by smell but no one is quite sure. By early November, most of the females are in oestrus and fighting among

ABOVE *The Beach at Gold Harbour, South Georgia, is jam packed with elephant seals. A creche of king penguin chicks lines the banks of a glacial melt stream.*

LEFT *Two bull elephant seals in the middle of a vicious fight over access to females. Pulling themselves up to their full height, the seals begin by threatening each other with loud roars. If this fails, fights break out that can last up to fifteen minutes and often result in serious injury to the combatants.*

the males reaches a peak. Then the beach is in tumult as high-ranking males mate constantly, stopping only occasionally to roar or fight. Males without harems lurk nearby, waiting for the chance to sneak up on a female. Sometimes, if the harem owner is totally engrossed and the female does not roar too much, a lower-ranking male may snatch a chance to make. But all too often, just as the interloper thinks success is close, the harem owner will come thundering over and see him off. A 4 tonne elephant seal can move at a surprising speed when sex is on his mind.

While all this is going on, some pups are still being born. Having left the warmth of the womb for the Antarctic cold, each new arrival is greeted by a flock of skuas and giant petrels. These scavengers of the south are keen to feast on fresh placenta and, if a mother is not careful, will go on to kill her young. The pup also finds itself on a battlefield, at constant risk of being trampled by fighting males. Its only refuge is its mother's nipple. For about 27 days after giving birth, the mother transfers a remarkable amount of energy to her pup through her milk. Each day the pup gains about 9 kilograms and gradually expands into a fat round ball that can hardly move. Meanwhile the mother loses 350 kilograms and becomes thin and exhausted. When the pups are less than four weeks old, their mothers return to the ocean to feed. The pups must then learn to swim and feed all by themselves, provisioned by their stores of fat.

Elephant seals spend only a tiny proportion of the year on the shore and are designed for life in the Southern Ocean. The layers of thick blubber that make them lumbering monsters on the beach provide perfect insulation for long periods at sea. Fish make up a quarter of their diet, but elephant seals specialize in feeding on squid. The South Georgia population is estimated to consume 3.5 million tonnes of squid a year. Their teeth are little more than widely spaced pegs and their eyes are especially adapted for searching out squid in the dark depths. The seals' retinas are rich in visual pigments that are particularly sensitive to the wavelengths of light emitted by the luminous organs of deep-sea squid. Recent experiments with electronic devices that record the time and depth of a seal's dives have shown that while at sea, elephant seals spend an extraordinary 80–90 percent of their lives under water. They can dive as deep as 1500 metres in search of their prey but most of their time is spent at depths of 200–400 metres. The time elephant seals pass on the surface is so short that it seems their muscles must work without oxygen for much of the dive – a feat that would give most of us severe muscle cramps.

While the elephant seal males are battling for their females, an altogether more graceful courtship is occurring above their heads. Almost all the hills above elephant seal beaches provide nesting sites for light-mantled sooty albatrosses. Half the size of a

A light-mantled sooty albatross soars on the updraughts along the cliffs of South Georgia.

wandering albatross, the sooty is perfectly elegant in flight. On its head, a subtle grey blends into a darker black and there is a brilliant crescent of white under each eye. No other bird is quite as gently beautiful. The male sooties choose a lonely nest site on a steep hillside covered with tussock grass and advertise for their mates. Soon the fiords of South Georgia echo with their eerie courtship call. As a female glides past on an updraught of wind, a male throws his head straight up in the air and gives a haunting two-part call. Time and again the female drifts past her prospective mate until finally his love song persuades her to land. Then, throwing their heads up to the sky and spreading their tail feathers in an elegant dance, the pair reaffirm a relationship that may have lasted for years. Eventually the birds take to the air for one of the most breathtaking courtship displays in nature. Feeling the wind with their long grey wings, the two birds circle their nest site in perfect harmony, each exactly matching the flight of its mate. Performed against a spectacular mountain backdrop, the sooty's aerial ballet is a beautiful celebration of spring. At last the sun has returned to melt the ice and fuel the ocean's food chain.

CHAPTER FOUR

THE SUN RETURNS

EVERY YEAR on 21 September the sun crosses the equator on its journey towards the southern hemisphere. It is a very significant day in the Antarctic year. Known as the spring equinox, it marks the end of the southern winter. After six months' absence the sun appears above the horizon at the South Pole. For scientists who have spent so long in almost complete darkness, it is a day of great rejoicing. During the six months that follow, the sun's return will have an enormous effect on the entire region, releasing the Antarctic from its great yoke of winter ice. At the start of September the sea ice is at its maximum extent, covering over 20 million square kilometres or about 57 percent of the surface of the Southern Ocean. By February the sun's heat has reduced the area of sea ice to just 4 million square kilometres and most of the ocean's vast area is accessible to the Antarctic's wildlife.

Only the sub-Antarctic islands, strung along the Polar Front like pearls, have remained ice free all winter. For them, spring is marked by more subtle changes than the retreat of sea ice. The sun's arrival stimulates the Southern Ocean's phytoplankton to bloom and soon the massive swarms of krill reform. With plenty of food available once again, other animals that have spent the winter foraging at sea come to the sub-Antarctic islands to breed. The cliff sides where wandering albatross chicks sat in lonely vigil fill up with a wide variety of other birds. Seals and penguins invade the beaches that were the sole preserve of the king penguins.

Among the first arrivals in September are the white-chinned petrels. They often return to find the ground still frozen and have to dig through thick snow to the burrows in which they nest. These large chicken-sized birds are all black apart from the tiny splash of white beneath the beak that gives them their name. They are also more affectionately known as shoemakers or singing cobblers after their courtship call, which

The return of the sun re-awakens the Antarctic Peninsula.

reminded early sealers and whalers of the noise made by a cobbler's sewing machine. This distinctive sound of the sub-Antarctic spring continues through the night as a pair sit close together outside their burrow, calling to each other. The burrow is cleverly designed to prevent flooding when the snow begins to thaw. A moat dug by the birds with their sharp claws surrounds a raised platform of earth and grass on which the single white egg is laid. So even when the burrow is full of water, the adult can incubate in the dry. In places so many shoemakers nest together that the soil is honeycombed with burrows and anyone walking across the colony is almost sure to fall through on to an irate bird.

White-chinned petrels nest among tussock grass, which is the characteristic and dominant vegetation of the sub-Antarctic. As spring progresses, the snowline often recedes up the hillsides as far as half a kilometre from the shoreline. On some sub-Antarctic islands such snow-free areas support several hundred species of plants. Most of them are mosses and lichens but there is always a handful of flowering plants. Of these, tussock grass is by far the most striking, covering most of the available soil near the shoreline and extending to an elevation of 250 metres. Tussock grows close together in thick clumps and can reach higher than a man. In the spring the clumps are often still covered in ice and walking through a field of tussock is rather like ice skating over the tops of large mushrooms. The hapless pedestrian is under constant threat of slipping into the narrow but deep channels between the tussock mounds and twisting an ankle. Though extremely difficult for animals on foot, tussock clumps provide an excellent habitat for nesting birds. Sheltered from the wind and the rain, the network of tunnels and caves beneath the tussock, and the clumps themselves, harbour many birds besides the white-chinned petrels.

In October the smaller albatrosses return to the tussock-covered hillsides, joining the wandering albatrosses that have been visiting their chicks all winter. The first back are the grey-headed albatrosses, half the weight of the wanderers. These handsome birds have a head washed with soft grey, a subtle smudge of black just around the eye which would impress any make-up artist and a beak edged with yellow turning to orange at the tip. They are soon joined by black-browed albatrosses which are a similar size to the grey-headeds and have the same smudge of black above the eye. The rest of their head is white and the beak is decorated with pink. Known as mollymawks, these two birds breed in colonies and often nest together on sheer hillsides that drop dramatically into the sea.

One of the greatest pleasures of the sub-Antarctic spring is to sit among the tussock as these birds return to their traditional nesting sites. Like all albatrosses,

ABOVE *A pair of white-chinned petrels display to each other at the mouth of their burrow among thick tussock grass on Bird Island. Their ceaseless calling is a very characteristic sound of the sub-Antarctic spring.*

LEFT *A calling white-chinned petrel tries to entice down a mate to its burrow among the tussock grass.*

THE SUB-ANTARCTIC ISLAND OF SOUTH GEORGIA

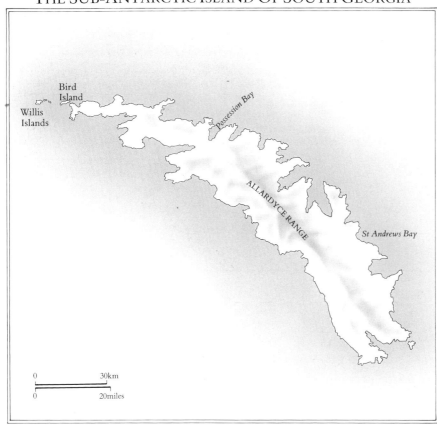

Bird
Island

Willis
Islands

Possession Bay

ALLARDYCE RANGE

St Andrews Bay

0   30km

0   20miles

*ABOVE A pair of grey-headed
albatrosses preen each other in a
ritual courtship that will reaffirm
their long-standing pair bond.*

*RIGHT Grey-headed albatrosses
return each year to traditional nest
sites among the tussock grass on
Bird Island. These are always on
steep cliff sides because the birds
need good strong updraughts to
take off.*

mollymawks are masters of their windy element. Playing on the updraught, they will often hang just centimetres from your face, feeling every tiny nuance of the wind with outstretched wings. After carefully surveying the colony in this way, the breeding pairs return to exactly the same nest they used the year before. Their simple mounds of mud and tussock survive from year to year but each season the albatrosses repair them with their beaks. Both species are monogamous, or faithful to one mate, and so courtship is quick and copulation usually takes place within a few days of the pair's arrival. After mating, and throughout the nesting period, the pair reaffirm their close relationship with mutual preening. The birds gently dress each other's feathers in what appears to be a state of complete bliss.

Although black-browed and grey-headed albatrosses seem at first sight to be very similar birds, they have quite different foraging and breeding strategies. The grey-headeds on South Georgia only manage to raise one chick every two years but the black-broweds are annual breeders. This may be partly explained by their different diets. Black-broweds eat mainly krill while grey-headeds feed mostly on cephalopods and, in the case of the South Georgian population, lampreys. Possibly the grey-headeds need longer to raise their chicks than the black-broweds because lampreys and cephalopods are harder to find than krill. The extra abundance of krill since people devastated whale populations earlier this century has probably provided a more reliable food source for the black-broweds.

The light-mantled sooty is the only other albatross that breeds in the Antarctic. Its diet consists largely of cephalopods and it, too, breeds only once every two years. While the grey-headeds and black-broweds nest in close colonies of up to tens of thousands of pairs, light-mantled sooties are more solitary breeders. Sometimes a handful will nest quite close together but often a pair will be all alone on a tussock-covered hilltop. Strongly territorial, light-mantled sooties defend their patch of coastline with beautiful eerie calls.

During the day the albatrosses fill the air and tussock with their noise and colour but at dusk another set of birds takes over the night shift. Around sunset, just out from the coast, great flocks of petrels start gathering on the surface of the sea. Sometimes thousands whirl round together in a grey smoke of birds. There are usually several different species in the flocks but they are all petrels and they all share a fear of skuas. The Antarctic has no birds of prey and, in many ways, the skuas take their place. These large gull-like birds, armed with a vicious hooked beak, are common residents on all the sub-Antarctic islands. Great aerial acrobats, they make their living by stealing chicks and taking smaller adults on the wing. While the larger white-chinned petrel is big enough to be able to return to its burrow in daylight, the smaller petrels must wait for the cover of darkness.

Climbing a steep hillside covered in tussock at night in the pitch black with a storm blowing is an extremely unpleasant experience. But on South Georgia in the spring it can also be a very rewarding one. At the right time of night, thousands and thousands of small petrels come rushing into their burrows. The air fills with calls and time and again soft wings brush your face. The birds are difficult to count because all are burrow nesters and the entrances to their nests are usually hidden deep in between the tussock. But many hillsides are so peppered with holes that they obviously occur in enormous numbers. The Antarctic is believed to have more than 150 million of these smaller petrels of the night, including an estimated 22 million dove prions breeding on South Georgia alone.

The blue petrel is the first to breed each year. Starting so early, it risks finding its burrow frozen over. To avoid this problem, the blue petrel returns regularly to its burrow during the winter to keep it open. Each of the smaller petrel species has its own special feeding technique. The smallest are the dumpy little diving petrels and, as their name suggests, they have specialized for diving and swimming under water. Their wings are reduced to tiny paddles that are presumably effective under water but make them rather comical in the air. Shooting out of the waves like tiny flying fish, they scuttle to their burrows, flapping their wings at a furious rate. The South Georgia diving petrel, one of the two diving petrels that breeds on South Georgia, has abandoned the tussock and hollows out burrows high above sea level in scree fields. Digging their way into hard gravel, these birds make a bare hillside resemble an enormous rabbit warren. Their numbers look particularly impressive because all the burrow entrances are clearly visible in this tower block of breeding birds.

The sounds of the Antarctic seldom include the dawn chorus familiar to people living in temperate areas. But South Georgia is home to the only song bird found south of the Polar Front, the South Georgia pipit. This small sparrow-sized bird lives a shy life skulking among the tussock. The mild microclimate in the gaps between the tussock clumps allows a thriving population of insects on which the pipits feed. In spring the pipits start to display, flying high up into the air and then, singing all the way, dropping like tiny parachutes to the ground. Listening to them among the tussock on a sunny day, it is difficult not to think of an English summer's day and just for a moment the Antarctic shows a gentler face.

Soon October is drawing to a close and the last of the sub-Antarctic's visitors, the Antarctic fur seals, are starting to return. Like the southern elephant seal, the

Antarctic fur seal is restricted largely to the sub-Antarctic islands. Ninety-five percent of its total world population breeds on South Georgia alone. Belonging to the same family as the sea lions, the fur seal looks rather like a large, misshapen dog, with heavy shoulders, a sleek tapering body and tiny, characteristic ears. It is a lively, alert animal and, lacking the heavy blubber of the elephant seal, is wonderfully sinuous and graceful as it twists and turns among the kelp. The fur seal's name comes from its dense coat, which provides insulation from the cold ocean. It is a clever adaptation of the typical mammalian two-layered coat. The outer layer consists of stiff guard hairs coated with water-repellent secretions. These protect and keep dry a much denser growth of fine fibres that trap a layer of insulating air. With roughly 40 000 hairs per square centimetre, the coat is one of the most effective natural defences against the rigours of the Southern Ocean and, ironically, led the Antarctic fur seal to the brink of extinction.

On 17 January 1775, Captain James Cook landed at Possession Bay in South Georgia and became the first man to see Antarctic fur seals on their breeding grounds. He wrote at the time 'seals, or sea bears, were pretty numerous'. His reports set in motion a hunt for fur seal pelts that very nearly wiped out the species. Within just 25 years, the sealing on South Georgia had reached a peak. In 1800–01 Edmund Fanning in the *Aspasia* took 57 000 fur seal skins and the total catch that summer was estimated at 112 000. After treatment, the pelts produced fine short-fibred fur which was in great demand throughout the nineteenth century for ladies' coats. By 1822, at least 1 200 000 fur seal skins had been taken from South Georgia alone and the species was virtually extinct there. It was the search for new fur seal populations that drove sealers further south and fuelled much of the early discovery of Antarctica.

At the start of this century, the Antarctic fur seal was a very rare animal indeed. A single young male sighted in South Georgia in 1916 was promptly killed. In 1931, when scientists on the British Discovery Expeditions found a small breeding population on Bird Island, the total world population was probably just a few hundred seals. But another example of humans' greedy exploitation of nature was already setting the scene for an amazing recovery. By the 1930s, the whaling industry, which was based in South Georgia, had reached a peak. By 1965, over 175 000 whales had been slaughtered round this island alone. Today less than 16 percent of the Southern Ocean's original whale population survives. Like most of the large baleen whales, the fur seals feed almost exclusively on krill. As whale numbers shrank, the krill increased dramatically and Antarctic fur seal populations gradually rose. At the end of the 1950s, fur seal numbers had reached about 5000. Throughout the 1960s, they increased at just over 16 percent

ABOVE LEFT A grey-headed albatross approaches its nest site on Bird Island.
BELOW LEFT With space at a premium, subordinate bull fur seals are forced into the sea.

a year and by 1976, the South Georgia population had reached 100 000. Today there are over 1 500 000 Antarctic fur seals and the population is still rising by nearly 10 percent a year. At this rate, the year 2000 may see an Antarctic fur seal population of over 4 million.

The enormous expansion in fur seal numbers is most evident when you visit the breeding beaches at the peak of the season. The thin strand of shingle between the sea and the tussock is so crowded with animals that it is extremely dangerous to walk among them. Male fur seals are highly aggressive at this time and anyone stupid enough to try and join them would soon get their legs ripped to bits by sharp seal teeth. Like the males of most land-breeding seals, the high-ranking male fur seals establish territories and breed with the females within them. As in elephant seals, size is the key factor in the males' ranking and this has led to an extraordinary difference in the size and shape of males and females. A full-grown male fur seal in breeding condition weighs up to 200 kilograms, about four times as much as a female. The thick set bull fur seal looks very much like a rugby prop forward, while his mate has all the makings of a timid wing three-quarter.

The males return first and start to establish territories on shingle beaches on the western end of South Georgia. Suitable flat beaches are rare and the rise in population has put a great pressure on space. The earlier males claim territories nearer the water's edge and initially these each cover about 60 square metres. But as more bulls arrive the territories gradually shrink until, at the peak of the breeding season, they are only about 22 square metres each. The battle for space is intense and as the pressure builds up, one can actually smell the aggression. Bull fur seals are stimulated to become aggressive during the breeding season by hormones which also produce an unmistakable musk.

All the disputes take place at the territory boundaries and the vast majority are settled by ritualized display. Two rival bulls face one another, rise up on their flippers, point their heads to the sky and give each other arrogant oblique stares. Then they quickly turn away from each other before resuming the head-high position. The tense situation is broken just occasionally by one of the bulls snatching or lunging at the other. True fights only break out when a newly arrived male tries to obtain territory from an already established bull. Starting with the ritualized head-high display, the dispute soon escalates into a vicious tussle as the two bulls push and bite each other. Sometimes one bull will get his teeth into the other, shaking and wrenching at its hide. The fight may last seconds or go on continuously for over five minutes until one of the rivals gives in and leaves the territory.

The females, or cows, start to arrive two or three weeks after the first males and

A young bull fur seal without his own territory on the breeding beach.

occupy the territories, 10 or so cows to a bull. By December the previously deserted beaches are packed with seals. The largest beach on South Georgia attracts a record 94 000 animals. On this spectacular battlefield, the successful males dominate the prize territories near the water's edge while less successful bulls are forced further up the beach and right up into the tussock. The lowest-ranking males have no territory at all and are forced to loiter in the shallows. Three or four times a day some will attempt a mad rush up the beach through a gauntlet of aggressive bulls in a desperate attempt to steal a patch of shingle. Few are successful and each season a number of males are killed in the attempt to secure a territory.

Two days after arriving on the beach, a female gives birth to the pup that was conceived the previous year. The births are highly synchronized, 90 percent of the pups being produced within a three-week period. Indeed, in one study, the date on which half the cows gave birth varied by only one day over a three-year period. Six or seven days after giving birth, a cow comes into oestrus and mates with the bull of her harem. Males near the shore achieve more copulations than their land-locked rivals further up the beach which explains why the shore sites are so heavily contested. Often within just a few minutes of mating, and never later than a few hours afterwards, the cow returns to the sea to feed.

After the births, the beaches appear crowded with pups and bulls but few females. The cows make repeated forays to sea, feeding there for days before returning to suckle their young. From late December onwards the cows tend to move their pups away from the shore to the relative peace of the tussock. This often involves them trekking several hundred metres from the shore and a hundred metres above sea level, but it is worth it to escape the beach battlefields. In densely populated colonies, over a quarter of pup deaths result from a female biting a strange pup that attempts to suckle. A further 11 percent are caused by pups being squashed or trampled by fighting bulls.

The cows suckle their pups for 117 days and during this period make about 17 feeding trips. Using modern electronics, scientists now know that the seals spend about 16 hours on their outward journeys in search of krill. On each trip they make on average about 400 dives, although the record is 902 dives. Usually the dives are less than 50 metres but occasionally the seals reach 200 metres. To provide for her own energy demands and to keep up her milk production, a cow fur seal must capture about 7 kilograms on each trip. The seals around South Georgia take large mature female krill which each weigh about 1 gram. So to suckle her pup, the cow fur seal must capture more than 6000 krill on every foray. Since a foraging trip takes her away for three to six days, she can only feed her pup intermittently. This makes the pups' growth rate

A fur seal mother protects her new-born pup.

slower than those of other seal species and, on South Georgia, pups born in late November are not weaned until early March.

Krill is also the favourite prey of the macaroni penguin. One of the smaller penguins, it gets its name from its dandy-like appearance, having a bright flash of yellow feathers on either side of its head. Like king penguins, macaronis are restricted to the sub-Antarctic region. However, they occur there in enormous numbers, accounting for 50 percent of the total biomass of seabirds in the sub-Antarctic. On South Georgia alone there are thought to be over 5 million pairs. Their preferred nesting sites are steep, bare rock faces with direct access to the sea and by early summer every suitable location is packed with squabbling macaroni penguins. The largest breeding population is on the Willis Islands, just off the north-western tip of South Georgia. These exposed rocky crags pierce the grey of the surrounding sea, climb abruptly and then disappear into an ever-present fog. Landing on the islands is extremely dangerous but from a boat you can see millions of mollymawks and penguins covering all the available space. Recent estimates suggest that these include 1–2 million macaronis.

The most impressive macaroni colony on Bird Island is on a single steep rock face which looks directly out over Stewart Strait towards the Willis Islands. The rock face is home to 80 000 pairs, one of the richest concentrations of life anywhere in the Antarctic, and from a vantage point in the tussock above the smell and noise of the birds are overpowering. To reach the colony the penguins have to swim up the appropriately named Macaroni Creek. This narrow passage between two steep cliffs faces west and is fully exposed to the prevailing swell. On rough days, massive waves squeeze up the creek, creating a permanent turmoil of white water. The breeding penguins have to come and go for food whatever the weather and during storms, they really show how tough animals have to be to survive in the Antarctic. Timid groups of 10 to 20 penguins will come porpoising up the creek and disappear momentarily in the chaos of breaking waves. Trying to coincide their landing with an incoming surge, the penguins will be thrown against the rocks time after time and bounce off like little black rubber balls. A couple may eventually make a landing only to be washed off again by the next incoming wave. As if the violent churning was not enough, young male fur seals constantly patrol the creek. Hidden by the white water, the seals will suddenly appear and grab unsuspecting penguins. For the penguins that do make it to the shore, the problems are far from over.

Again, the males arrive first at the colony and the females follow. Within just two weeks, a previously empty hillside is jammed with tens of thousands of noisy birds. Of all the penguins, the macaroni must be the most vocal and aggressive. Each new

Over hundreds of years the claws of climbing macaroni penguins have worn grooves in the rocks.

male arriving at the bottom of the colony has to run a very painful gauntlet to reach the tiny patch of rock that will become his nest site. Already established males peck violently at any passing bird and sometimes vicious fights break out. Then two males grab each other tightly with their beaks and, calling loudly, often end up tumbling down the slope locked in intense combat. If a penguin's nest happens to be at the top of the slope, the unfortunate bird may have to endure an hour's pecking before he finds his own quiet spot. By the time the females start trickling back, the males are already in place. The females too have to undergo an ordeal by beak to reach their mate. But once reunited, the pair stand touchingly close, putting one flipper behind each other's back. Then two birds that have just been violent and noisy start quietly preening each other with intimate pleasure.

Macaronis are members of a family of crested penguins which contains seven species. Four of these are restricted to New Zealand and its sub-Antarctic islands. All the crested penguins look rather similar and share an intriguing breeding strategy. They lay two eggs, the first of which is smaller than the second and rarely hatches. The difference in egg size is particularly great in macaronis whose first egg is less than half the size of the second and virtually never hatches. The question that obviously arises is: why does the macaroni waste energy laying two eggs when it only ever succeeds with one? Often the first egg is lost to predators or damaged by rivals before the second egg is even laid. Macaronis are such aggressive birds that frequently an egg is lost during squabbles. It has been suggested that the first egg is an insurance against the loss of the more important second egg. Unfortunately, this argument fails because the first egg seldom manages to hatch. Possibly macaronis used to lay two viable eggs and are now moving towards laying a single egg, but scientists studying this bird remain puzzled.

South Georgia has one other breeding penguin, the gentoo, and this bird has adopted a very different lifestyle from the macaroni. The gentoo penguin is larger than the macaroni and far more docile, a relaxed, almost laid-back bird. Its black head has two characteristic white patches above the eyes and its bill is a sharp pink dagger. Norwegian whalers used to call gentoos 'tussock penguins' because, unlike the macaronis, they nest among the tussock. Often their colonies are quite high up steep hillsides which are still snow-covered in spring. With extraordinary determination, the gentoos waddle slowly up the slopes making obvious pathways in the snow. They scoop out little hollows in the ground and industriously collect small stones and scraps of vegetation to line the cup. In this nest they lay two eggs and, unlike those of the macaronis, both hatch. Gentoos do take krill but small fish also form an important part of their diet.

PREVIOUS PAGE A macaroni penguin returning to its nest runs the gauntlet of its neighbours.
LEFT Aggressive macaroni penguins space their nests carefully but fill every bit of bare ground.

This makes them mainly inshore feeders while the macaronis usually go far offshore in search of krill.

The total gentoo population is somewhere between 250 000 and 300 000 pairs, about a third of which breed on South Georgia. While macaronis are restricted almost entirely to the sub-Antarctic islands, gentoos range much further south. They nest on maritime islands and even on the Antarctic Peninsula right down to 65 degrees south. The southern race is smaller with shorter flippers, bill and feet than the South Georgia birds. The hardy southern birds have to wait until the sea ice retreats before they can reach their nesting sites. So while on South Georgia the first gentoo eggs are laid in mid to late October, the birds on the Antarctic Peninsula do not lay until around about a month later.

The spring equinox often marks the start of the sea ice's retreat. The sun's return across the equator coincides with a period of violent storms and gales. Powerful waves erode the edge of the sea ice and the sun's heat starts the melt. Layers of pigmented algae that have grown slowly in the ice throughout the winter help absorb the sun's radiation, speeding up a process that can melt ice 2–3 metres thick in just six weeks. The algae released from the ice make an important contribution to the start of the food chain, further accelerating the summer pulse of life. By mid-November most of the maritime islands are free of ice. Midway between the mild sub-Antarctic islands and permanently frozen Antarctica, the maritime islands are also important habitats for breeding birds and seals. Although they lack the extensive vegetation and soils of the sub-Antarctic, they do provide large areas of precious snow-free rock vital to nesting birds. The close proximity of the Southern Ocean in the summer produces a climate milder than that on most of Antarctica. The exception is the long arm of the Antarctic Peninsula which, though strictly part of Antarctica, stretches far to the north and so is also largely ice free in summer with a basically maritime climate.

Almost all the maritime islands lie along a submarine ridge, the Scotia Arc. This forms a huge eastward-extending loop linking the Andes of South America with the mountain range of the Antarctic Peninsula. The biggest group of maritime islands and the largest archipelago in the Antarctic is the 540 kilometre chain of the South Shetland Islands. Most are tiny, remote pinpricks of rock in a vast expanse of open ocean. Geologically young and often volcanic, their rocky landscapes have been shaped by glaciers, icecaps and the constant erosive power of waves. They are about as far removed as it is possible to get from the oceanic island ideal. Yet very few are deserted and some provide home for literally millions of birds.

Like South Georgia, the maritime islands are nesting sites for enormous numbers

ABOVE Gentoo penguins guard their young chicks on Couverville Island. Here on the Antarctic Peninsula the only available nesting material is small stones.

BELOW The early whalers who first came across gentoo penguins on South Georgia called them tussock penguins because that is where they nest on the northerly sub-Antarctic Islands.

FOLLOWING PAGE As summer progresses, the sea ice along the Antarctic Peninsula gradually breaks up into loose pack and allows the wildlife to return to their breeding grounds.

of petrels. These birds belong to an order, the Procellariiformes, which also includes fulmars, shearwaters and albatrosses. The birds in the order, excluding the larger albatrosses, split quite neatly into two according to their nesting strategy. The smaller species – the prions, diving petrels, gadfly petrels, storm petrels and shearwaters – tend to nest in burrows and return to feed their chicks at night. Because they have to have soil in which to make their burrows, they are restricted to the more northerly sub-Antarctic islands. The larger petrels – the cape petrel, Antarctic fulmar, snow petrels and Antarctic petrel – all about the size of a pigeon, only need a rocky ledge to breed on. This is readily available on the maritime islands and further south wherever there is snow-free rock. The larger species choose ledges on inaccessible cliffs which tend to be swept clear of snow by the wind early in the season and so these birds can generally start breeding earlier than the smaller petrels. Often they breed synchronously in quite staggering numbers. A colony of Antarctic petrels on one lonely rocky outcrop in East Antarctica, Scullin Monolith, contains at least 157 000 breeding pairs. There are so many circling the colony at any one time that the monolith seems permanently covered in a thick mist of birds.

The Antarctic petrels and snow petrels will make long journeys inland to find suitable rocky nesting ledges. For many seasoned hands, the snow petrel is the Antarctic's most beautiful bird, a real symbol of the deep south. This all-white bird with a black eye and beak is usually seen associated with ice or icebergs. Snow petrel nests have been found right in the interior of Antarctica, in one case more than 180 kilometres from the coast. The icecap that covers the continent is several kilometres thick but in a few places the tops of large mountain ranges pierce through the engulfing ice. It is to these isolated mountain summits, or nunataks, that snow petrels fly in search of precious bare rock. They bring life to what must be the most lifeless part of the planet. Their choice of nest site is particularly remarkable given that the adults must constantly return to the distant ocean to find food for their chicks.

Like most petrels, the larger species feed principally on krill and other crustaceans. They gather their food from the surface of the water, usually not far from the edge of the pack ice. While following humpback whales feeding on krill, we found that large flocks of cape petrels had learnt to profit from them. Most of the krill was too far below the surface for the petrels but the whales kept driving clumps up within their reach. Every time the whales moved on the petrels followed, making it possible to track a distant pair of feeding whales by the telltale flock. Apart from crustaceans, these southern petrels also feed their chicks on a rich oil secreted into the stomach by

ABOVE RIGHT Chinstrap penguins rest on icebergs before returning to a nearby colony.
BELOW RIGHT Snow petrels fly far to the south but often breed deep in the Antarctic Continent.

special cells. The oil seems to provide a concentrated energy source which can be carried more conveniently over the long distances from the foraging grounds. It also has another use. Both adults and chicks are able to forcefully eject the oil from their crops up to 2 metres from the nest. This provides an excellent defence against skuas or gulls which, if drenched in the oil, would lose the insulation of their plumage. The foul-smelling oil is also a very effective deterrent against humans keen to interfere with the nest, as many scientists have learnt to their cost.

Wilson's storm petrel seems a remarkably fragile bird to survive in the south. Yet this tiniest of petrels, weighing just 30–40 grams, has one of the largest ranges of all Antarctic birds. It manages to do this by deviating from the general pattern of petrel breeding strategies. In the north, on the sub-Antarctic islands, it breeds like all the other small petrels in a burrow in the soil. But in the south it makes do with a tiny crevice in broken rock in which it struggles down to find a sheltered corner. Wilson's storm petrels can breed as far south as 76 degrees and often return in spring to find their traditional nesting sites covered in snow. At twilight in their colonies, the birds perform a gentle aerial ballet just above the ground. Spreading the webs of their tiny feet, they reveal flashes of yellow skin while calling to each other all the time. Eventually a male will squeeze down between the rocks and snow to the chamber below but his muffled call can still be heard, enticing the female to join him.

The maritime Antarctic has one penguin all of its own. The total world population of chinstrap penguins is estimated to be about 6.5 million and all but about 10 000 nest on the Antarctic Peninsula or the maritime islands nearby. At just over 4 kilograms, the chinstrap is smaller and more slender than the gentoo. It gets its name from a thin line of black feathers that form a strap across the top of its otherwise white breast. Of all the penguins, chinstraps are the greatest climbers and seem to nest in the highest, rockiest places. Using their beaks and their sharp claws they can pull themselves up extraordinarily steep slopes and often end up hundreds of metres above sea level.

By far the largest numbers of chinstraps breed on the remote South Sandwich Islands to the north of the Weddell Sea. On one of these active volcanoes, Zavodovski Island, there are thought to be 2 million penguins but no one has ever been able to count them accurately. Another active volcano, Deception Island in the South Shetland archipelago, also has an impressive chinstrap colony. The black and white penguins make a striking sight arranged against the black volcanic ash of its steep slopes. The volcano last erupted in 1971 and the island still has hot springs, fumaroles and steaming beaches. All these assist the nesting penguins by helping to melt the snow early. The

On Horseshoe Island off the Antarctic Peninsula
the rocks are patterned with copper carbonate.

largest of Deception's chinstrap colonies covers the side of a caldera at Baily Head. The steep black slope of volcanic ash curves round to provide a dramatic amphitheatre for 120 000 pairs of penguins.

Chinstraps are very aggressive birds and carefully arrange their nests a clear pecking distance from each other. Like gentoos they lay two eggs but their breeding is not synchronized between different locations nor even within colonies. The chinstraps' habit of choosing nesting sites high up mountain slopes seems to leave them very much at the mercy of the winter snow. They cannot start to lay until the snow has thawed and this happens at different rates in different years and at different places. The more established birds claim the more accessible locations where the snow usually melts first. On Deception, the younger birds have to make an enormous trek up to the very top of the volcano, disappearing away into the mist. For some the journey from beach to nest takes over 90 minutes. Most of the birds have to waddle along one narrow riverside and, at the peak of the breeding season, so many birds are using the route that they look like rush-hour commuters racing for their trains.

By the end of October, when the chinstraps start returning to their traditional colonies, the sea ice has retreated far enough south to release the maritime islands and much of the Antarctic Peninsula. But further south the region is still largely frozen and it will be January or February before the ice reduces to its minimum extent. For another penguin this represents a major problem. The Adélie is the penguin of the deep south. It is smaller than most and has a blue-black head and chin, pure white underbelly and distinctive white-lidded eyes. More than any other penguin, it inspires anthropomorphic thoughts with its tidy little dinner suit and droll, rolling gait. Yet the Adélie is remarkably tough and perfectly adapted for the harsh conditions it must endure. Underneath an exceptionally thick pelt of dense feathers, it has a substantial layer of subcutaneous fat. This provides insulation and an energy reserve for the birds to draw on during long periods without food. The short bill is uniquely feathered along half its length and the external nares are kept tightly closed to reduce loss of body heat. All these adaptations have enabled the Adélie to breed further south than most other birds and become the most numerous penguin in Antarctica.

While most penguins only nest on the islands or the Antarctic Peninsula, the Adélies breed at over 50 locations on the continent itself. The most southerly colony is just 1300 kilometres from the South Pole at Cape Royds at 77 degrees South, a lonely outpost of 2000 pairs. The largest colony is 71 degrees South at Cape Adare. It covers many square kilometres and contains an estimated 220 000 pairs which make so much noise they can be heard 50 kilometres downwind. Nesting so far south, all the

PREVIOUS PAGE Chinstrap penguins return to the black volcanic beaches of Deception Island.

THE ANTARCTIC PENINSULA AND THE ISLANDS OF THE SCOTIA SEA

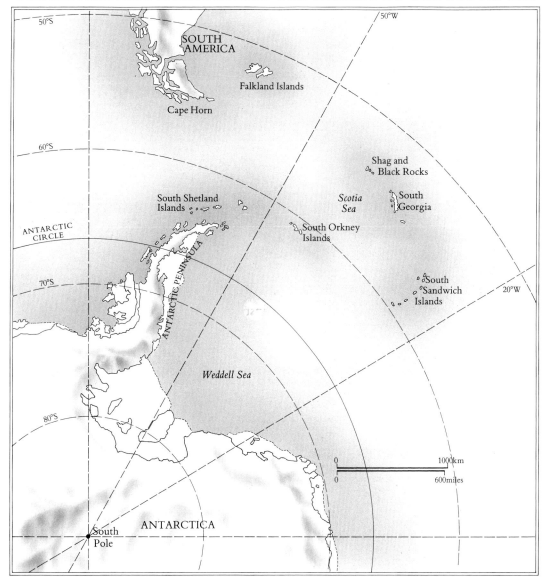

Adélies face the same problem. When they have to return from the ocean to breed there is still a great deal of sea ice between them and their nest sites. Waiting for this to melt would waste valuable time in a very short summer and so the penguins are forced to walk. It is an extraordinary sight to see a lonely file of Adélies marching resolutely on with their curious rolling gait. In some years their journeys over the ice are in excess of 100 kilometres, though 20 to 40 kilometres is more usual. Whatever the distance, their appearance signals that even in the deep south the Antarctic winter is finally over.

CHAPTER FIVE

THE RACE TO BREED

Summer in the Antarctic is a short time of plenty. The return of the sun to the southern hemisphere bathes much of the continent in 24 hour daylight. The sea ice, which reflected back most of this radiation during the winter, gradually retreats. The exposed ocean absorbs the sunlight and a great pulse of energy surges through the food chain. Phytoplankton blooms provide food for swarms of krill and other zooplankton and soon a great wave of animals heads south. The whales that spent the Antarctic winter breeding in temperate waters follow the retreating ice to enjoy their first meal in months. Islands that were trapped in ice are suddenly set free and every centimetre of bare rock they have to offer is quickly grabbed by nesting birds and seals. The first precious drops of freshwater are released by melting ice and Antarctica's sparse vegetation can grow again. The Antarctic summer comes as quickly as it goes and all the wildlife knows that the race to breed is on.

Nowhere is the change more noticeable than along the Antarctic Peninsula. For many, this is the most beautiful part of the Antarctic, unlocked each year by the retreating ice. Above 70 degrees South, and particularly on its milder western side, the Peninsula provides some of the continent's gentlest conditions. In summer, temperatures can reach up to zero degrees centigrade, and rain replaces snow. It is on this rocky backbone stretching north that most of the continent's wildlife survives. As the ice retreats, it releases a chain of islands and inlets in the Peninsula. Protected from the open ocean to the west, the waters between these islands are often mirror calm,

A crabeater seal hauled out on an ice floe.

reflecting in their surface the nearby mountain peaks. Almost every patch of accessible bare rock is covered in a penguin colony. Even tiny crags that pierce the mountainsides are used by nesting birds.

By the time the Adélie penguin eggs hatch, towards the end of December, it is essential that the sea ice has broken up far south enough to allow the adults immediate access to the sea. Adélies choose their nest sites on the basis of two important criteria. They always go for exposed places where they can be sure the wind will have blown away the winter snows by the start of the breeding season. And they never nest further south than the edge of the sea ice at its summer minimum. Though Adélies can manage a walk over ice at the start of the season and when they are incubating, they must have easy access to the sea and food as soon as there are hungry chicks.

All the smaller southern penguins – the Adélies, gentoos and chinstraps – have a very similar breeding cycle. They return to the same colony each year and often settle within centimetres of last year's nest. For the following two to three weeks there is intense activity as nests are built, and courtship and copulation take place. The nests are usually no more than simple hollows lined with stones and any other little bits of bone or vegetation the birds can find. Penguins are great kleptomaniacs and there are often heated disputes over stolen nesting material. The colonies become even more noisy as the birds perform striking vocal and visual courtship displays. Adélies raise their heads in the air, sway from side to side and cackle at each other. Chinstraps throw their beaks up in the air and let out ear-splitting calls, sounding rather like angry donkeys. Even the more peaceful gentoos have an elaborate ritual of calls and postures.

The birds quieten down a little once their two eggs have been laid. Usually male gentoo and Adélie penguins undertake the first incubation shift which lasts about two weeks. The poor chinstrap female covers the first 6 to 10 days herself and so has the ordeal of up to 30 days onshore without feeding on top of producing two large, energy-demanding eggs. After the initial incubation period, the female and male of all the species take turns to incubate the eggs while the other feeds at sea. About seven weeks after being laid, the eggs hatch. At first the tiny, down-covered chicks are very susceptible to cold and the parents must brood them to keep them warm. Well-fed Adélie chicks put on about 100 grams per day and after two weeks or so are large enough to control their body temperature and wander freely from the parents. By the third week most have joined creches within a few metres of their nest sites. These informal huddles provide the chicks with some protection from the worst of the weather and predators, freeing the parents to forage at sea so doubling the chicks' food supply.

PREVIOUS PAGE A chinstrap penguin nurses its newly-hatched chick out of the egg.
RIGHT An Adélie penguin regurgitates krill to its two-week-old chicks.

Penguin colonies become very busy places as parents come and go to supply their hungry chicks. The adults usually go to sea for about 24 hours. Most set off in the morning and tend to return close together at the end of the day, creating something of a rush hour. This pattern is especially marked in the more northerly colonies where for much of the summer there is actually a night. Since penguins catch their prey by sight they prefer to hunt in daylight and as dusk approaches, are continually returning to the colony in groups of 10 or 20. From the shore, these bands seem to appear from nowhere, porpoising in between the icebergs and it is difficult not to wonder where they have been. Such knowledge is also important for conservation, since penguins make up 90 percent of the biomass of Antarctic birds, and recently scientists have been finding out about their foraging strategies.

Chinstraps and Adélies feed almost exclusively on krill. Both species bring back about 300 grams each trip and a pair will feed their chicks on average once a day. How far they travel for food varies a great deal with location. A distance of 20–30 kilometres is typical but there are reports of Adélies going 238 kilometres from their colony and chinstraps as far as 264 kilometres. When they eventually find the krill swarms, chinstraps and Adélies make $1\frac{1}{2}$ minute dives, usually to less than 45 metres. However chinstraps do reach 70 metres and the record Adélie dive is 175 metres. On each dive they catch about 16 krill. Adélies tend to take smaller krill than chinstraps, perhaps because Adélies start breeding earlier when the krill itself is still growing. But even when both species are feeding at the same time, the difference in prey size still persists. Where chinstraps occur they almost always overlap with Adélies, and it may be that competition with chinstraps forces the Adélies to feed off the smaller krill.

Unlike the other two, gentoos take small fish as well as krill and they seem to have developed two different diving patterns to catch their different prey. When they are after krill they generally do quick bounce dives, spending little time at depth swimming horizontally. When hunting fish they make longer flat-bottomed dives and search along the seabed. The latter dives are more energy demanding and become increasingly inefficient at greater depths. So gentoos tend to keep their dive depth to a minimum by fishing in shallower inshore waters.

The break up of the sea ice in summer allows another fisherman to extend its range a long way down the Antarctic Peninsula. The blue-eyed shag is the only member of the cormorant family that breeds south of the Polar Front. It has a wide distribution in the southern hemisphere, occurring from the coasts of Chile and Argentina down to 68 degrees South. The shag never fishes far away from its nest and so was a great favourite with early Antarctic explorers scouring the vast expanse of the Southern

Ocean for clues to undiscovered lands. In 1916, when Ernest Shackleton made his incredible journey in a tiny canvas boat from the tip of the Antarctic Peninsula across 1450 kilometres of open ocean, it was fishing shags that alerted him to his first landfall on South Georgia. The birds that breed on the Peninsula are particularly striking. The white belly is topped with a shiny blue-black back and head, a bright blue ring surrounds each eye and the base of the long-hooked beak has orange growths which become especially bright in the breeding season.

Blue-eyed shag nesting colonies are smelly, noisy, amusing places. The majority contain less than 100 pairs but in some spots the birds congregate in very large numbers. Between the Falkland Islands and South Georgia are some isolated crags, appropriately called Shag Rocks, over 250 kilometres away from the nearest island of South Georgia. The tiny cluster of rocks in the middle of the ocean is home to little else except thousands of blue-eyed shags, so inaccessible that nobody has managed to count them. Uniquely among Antarctic birds, shags use their so-called rookeries all year round, roosting there at night throughout the winter. This means they are never too far from open water, where they feed principally on fish.

Shags build large traditional nests using their guano to cement together a strange collection of seaweed, lichens and mosses. All these building materials are in very short supply and if a pair leave their nest for even a moment, a rival will fly in and start frantically stealing them. While squabbling over material is still going on, courtship begins. The birds' long necks dance together, rather like two charmed snakes, as the shags put their cheeks side by side and bow, and then swap over cheeks and bow again. After mating and incubation, the young that finally hatch out are the only Antarctic chicks born naked. This means that the hatchlings cannot regulate their own temperature and must rely on their parents for warmth. In bad weather there is enormous chick loss but shags are long-lived birds and have many chances to breed.

The two parents forage for their chicks at different times of day, possibly to avoid competition between the sexes. The females tend to leave at sunrise and return around midday. Then the males take over and usually continue fishing until sunset. Like gentoo penguins, shags hunt by sight, mainly in shallower, inshore waters, and catch their prey by pursuit diving. But while the penguins spend 50 percent of their foraging time diving, shags only need to be under water for 20 percent of the time. They do more deep dives than the gentoos, their record depth being 116 metres. Unlike the penguins, the shags use their powerful webbed feet to help them travel deeper. When each parent returns to the nest, the chicks feed hungrily on the catch. As they get larger, the greedy chicks stick their beaks right into the parent's long snake-like neck to reach the food in the gullet. The shag's sharp dagger-like beak makes the process look like the ultimate sword-swallowing trick.

The blue-eyed shag is restricted by sea ice to the northerly reaches of the Peninsula. South of about 70 degrees the Peninsula is very like the rest of Antarctica, dominated by ice and snow, and just eight flying birds manage to breed there. Even the relatively mild northern Peninsula has only 13 breeding species of flying birds. Given how very few bird species can survive the demanding climate, it is not surprising that the shag is the cormorant family's sole representative in the Antarctic. Similarly, only one true gull breeds in the Antarctic region, the Dominican or kelp gull. Closely resembling the greater black-backed gull of the northern hemisphere, it is a large black and white bird with a yellow beak that bears a bright red spot in the breeding season. Like the blue-eyed shag, it occurs widely throughout the southern hemisphere and nests on the Peninsula as far south as Marguerite Bay at 68 degrees South.

The exact distribution of kelp gulls on the Peninsula is directly related to the occurrence of their main prey, limpets. The gulls hunt these molluscs, the only large, abundant invertebrates available to them, between the high- and low-tide marks. The males start to gather just as the tide is about to turn. Sitting in water less than a metre deep, they get at the limpets by plunging down and sometimes completely submerging themselves in water. As the tide continues to fall, more and more males arrive, and eventually the females join in at low tide, the best limpet-catching time. This sexual difference in foraging technique only occurs in the early stages of breeding. As soon as the chicks have hatched, the females join the males throughout the low-tide cycle. It seems that when there is less demand for food the females only bother to hunt at the optimum time but when there are hungry chicks both parents have to work hard. Although the parents supplement their chicks' limpet diet with small fish, limpets remain the key to the kelp gull's breeding success. Unless the male can keep his mate well supplied during the vital courtship and egg-laying period, clutches will be small. The gulls take in the limpets whole and later regurgitate the crushed shells. Great middens of shells lie all around the nesting colonies, providing ample evidence of the close reliance of gull on mollusc.

While kelp gulls and blue-eyed shags only nest on the Peninsula and islands further north, one smaller, fragile-looking seabird manages to breed further south. The Antarctic tern, the continent's only breeding tern, is a delicate white and silver-grey bird with a striking blood-red dagger of a bill. Though most of its population is restricted to the Scotia Sea area, the tern has a circumpolar presence. Its diet consists mainly of small crustaceans and fish, and it is particularly fond of feeding along the

RIGHT *Blue-eyed shags preen each other as part of an elaborate courtship ritual. During the breeding season the colour of the nasal growth intensifies.*

BELOW *Kelp gulls gather on rocks near their breeding sites on Couverville Island. The kelp gull is the only Antarctic gull and their range is closely tied to the range of their favourite prey — limpets.*

front of glaciers. These massive rivers of ice, which can reach 100 metres high, are constantly advancing and calving enormous blocks of ice straight into the sea. When large sections of ice break off, they produce splashes of impressive noise and size. They also create tidal waves big enough to sink a small ship and bring a lot of krill and other crustaceans up to the surface. The terns have learnt to exploit this chance and can often be seen fluttering along the face of a mighty glacier.

Antarctic terns nest in little scraps of rock out in the open. This makes them very exposed to both the weather and predators. They see off the latter with brave, aggressive behaviour, as anyone who has walked too close to a tern's nest will know. The birds attack with great spirit, swooping down to try to peck the intruder's head and calling frantically. Even if a predator does steal eggs or chicks, the terns have the ability, rare in Antarctic birds, to lay again and have a second or even third attempt at successful breeding. The Antarctic terns are resident in the region all year round and courtship displays start in the middle of winter. They begin to defend a future nest site while it is still completely snow-covered and some birds lay so early that their eggs crack with the cold. The intense effort to breed continues throughout the summer and the birds may lay right up to the beginning of February, when most other Antarctic birds have large chicks. This greatly extended breeding season may help to avoid competition between the terns at the crucial times of chick-rearing and the later adult moult. Also, by not producing their chicks synchronously, the terns may reduce the pressure of predators on their young.

During the summer the Antarctic tern is joined by its northern counterpart, the Arctic tern. Probably the greatest of all bird migrants, the Arctic tern flies each year over 12 000 kilometres from its breeding grounds in the high Arctic right down to within the Antarctic Circle. It spends the southern summer feeding on the Antarctic's rich harvest and then makes the same journey in reverse to exploit the Arctic's bounty in the northern summer. By fitting in two summers at high latitudes in any one year, it manages to spend three-quarters of its life in nearly continuous daylight. Since terns hunt by sight, this enables the Arctic tern to feed round the clock for most of its life. It only sees the sun actually set during the two brief periods it is on passage through the tropics. The Arctic tern's journeys are extraordinary feats of endurance and make it all the more remarkable that the Antarctic tern, which is almost indistinguishable from its Arctic cousin, hardly migrates at all.

The heat of summer does not only break up the sea ice. It also melts some of the snow and ice on land to produce the rarest and most precious commodity in Antarctica – fresh water. Though 90 percent of the world's fresh water is found in

PREVIOUS PAGE Feeding kelp gulls are dwarfed by an iceberg.

ABOVE *An Antarctic tern pulls its primary feathers through its beak as part of a regular preening session.*

LEFT *An Antarctic tern returns to its nest with freshly caught krill.*

Antarctica, most of it remains permanently frozen and unavailable to life. The seals and seabirds are specially adapted to get the water they need from their food or the sea but all Antarctic plants must have fresh water at some stage in their lives. The scarcity of vegetation in the region is largely due to the very low humidity, together with the extremely cold temperatures and the almost complete absence of soil. Those plants that do survive cling to protected rock faces which become warm enough in summer to produce trickles of melt water.

Scientists who have spent a couple of years working in Antarctica are amazed on their return home to see trees again. Even on South Georgia there are no woody plants at all, not even the tiniest shrub. Excluding the sub-Antarctic islands, the landscape is almost entirely white. Black rock breaks through in a few places but green is the colour of dreams. Into this black and white world summer brings the occasional, rare splash of colour. In places hundreds of metres of snow bank are covered in red, as if some dreadful blood-letting has taken place. These brilliant flashes of colour are caused by the simplest plants of all, single-celled algae. The bright colour comes from pigments the algae use to photosynthesize and these may be red, green or, occasionally, yellow. The algae live in snow that becomes saturated with melt water during the summer. This only occurs in the milder areas, along the coast of the continent and, in particular, along the western edge of the Antarctic Peninsula.

Apart from algae, the only plants that occur in any variety in Antarctica are the mosses, lichens, liverworts and fungi. Of these, the most widespread and hardy are the lichens. They are the most southerly growing plants on the planet, having been found at 86 degrees South, just 445 kilometres from the South Pole. They owe their hardiness to a high concentration of proteins and acids which do not freeze until at least minus 20 degrees centigrade. A lichen is made up of an alga and a fungus combined in a mutually beneficial relationship. The alga can photosynthesize and so provide energy for the partnership while the fungus provides protection, moisture and nutrients. The resultant lichen can photosynthesize at a lower temperature than all other plants and with very little light or moisture. It is also able to live totally without soil, extracting all the nutrients it needs from bare rock. This allows lichens to survive on isolated nunataks in the middle of an otherwise lifeless icecap. The occasional snow petrel or skua may visit in the summer, but otherwise lichens are almost the only life form to survive there year round.

In the harsh main part of the continent the total number of lichen species is 125 and this rises to 150 along the Peninsula and the nearby islands. By far the most spectacular displays are found on the South Shetland and South Orkney Islands where

Summer warmth is just sufficient to melt ice and release precious fresh water.

large areas of rock are completely covered with a bright orange, yellow or red crust. Though the majority of Antarctic species stay flat against the rocks, there are also bushy and leafy lichens. These grow into tiny bushes and trees that cover the rocks in a grey beard. All the precious lichen growths have to be treated with great care. Most lichens only increase by about 15 millimetres every 100 years, so a clumsy movement could destroy many centuries of growth.

Once lichens are established, they can provide a starting point for mosses. These plants are almost as tough as lichens but they cannot grow without a little sandy soil. As a result they are far less widespread with a total of only 30 species in most of Antarctica, rising to 85 if the Peninsula and nearby islands are included. Moss reproduction occurs so rarely in the Antarctic that scientists have never seen it happen in some species. For most of the year mosses simply endure the cold and do not even grow. However in the summer, the temperature on exposed rock may reach as high as 40 degrees centigrade and under these conditions moss carpets grow well. Again the most splendid examples are found along the western Peninsula and on the nearby archipelagos. The dead moss shoots and rhizomes can slowly accumulate and form peat banks which may be up to several metres thick and thousands of years old. Like that of the lichens, moss growth is measured in centuries rather than years and a careless footstep in a moss bank will remain there for hundreds of years.

The rarest plants of all in the Antarctic are the flowering plants. Even South Georgia has only 26 native species. In comparison, in the midlands of Britain, for example, which lie on the same latitude in the northern hemisphere, are home to thousands of species. Antarctica itself has just two flowering plants and both of them are restricted to the northern Peninsula. Neither really looks like a flowering plant, having minute, inconspicuous, drab blooms. The most common is an Antarctic hairgrass, *Deschampsia antarctica*, which has been found right down to just over 68 degrees South. It needs the soil created by lichens and moss and, while the South Orkney and South Shetland Islands have some luxuriant growths, on the continent it occurs only as little low patches in well-sheltered spots. The Peninsula's other flowering plant is a little pink known as colobanthus (*Colobanthus quitensis*) which grows in compact little cushions just 25 centimetres across. Both these plants need nutrients as well as moisture and soil, and tend to grow around nesting birds whose guano provides the basic nutrients essential for plant life. Mosses and lichens flourish there too, producing the soil on which the flowering plants can grow. A lone kelp gull, nesting many kilometres from any other bird, can be the basis of a tiny plant community of mosses, lichens and Antarctic hairgrass. Without the gull, there would just be bare rock.

Lichen encrusts the rocks on Couverville Island.

ABOVE *Single-celled algae can survive in snow and each summer, as melting releases freshwater, complete hillsides can be daubed with unexpected colours – red, green, and occasionally, yellow.*

LEFT *The Antarctic hairgrass,* Deschampsia antarctica, *grows among a small clump of moss. Rarely more than a few centimetres tall, this grass is one of only two flowering plants that survive on the Antarctic continent.*

The miniature forests of moss and lichen provide a hunting ground for many of Antarctica's land animals. No land vertebrates can survive the winter on the continent and the only land animals that remain there all year round are invertebrates. The region pushes its invertebrates, like all its wildlife, to the edge of their tolerance and the land invertebrates seldom occur in large numbers nor is the variety of species great. The biggest factor limiting their distribution is not the cold but the constant threat of drying out. Antarctica's isolated position in the Southern Ocean means that its land animals cannot migrate to escape the deep freeze of winter. Most remain dormant in the soil during this time, surviving on traces of moisture which are maintained in the soil by a layer of permafrost.

The thick moss carpets on the Peninsula and the islands of the Scotia Arc provide moisture for a variety of tiny animals and it is there that the most complex land food chain occurs. Starting the chain are single-celled protozoans at a density of up to 900 million per square metre. They and the moss are eaten by microscopic creatures called rotifers which are especially common in damp moss. There are 29 species of nematodes, or roundworms, which eat plants and protozoans and themselves fall prey to predatory fungi. The Peninsula also has 17 representatives of the plant-eating tardigrades. These tiny, flat-bodied, slow-moving creatures have been found as far south as 77 degrees.

A powerful microscope is needed to view Antarctica's Serengeti – a moss carpet filled with mites and springtails. Lying further up the food chain, these are the dominant land invertebrates in Antarctica. Mites have eight legs, like their relatives the spiders, and look like tiny brightly coloured spiders. Of those that live among the moss, some are herbivores while some are carnivores, preying on other mites and springtails. In places they can be extremely numerous and one species common on the Peninsula, *Alaskozetes antarcticus*, forms clusters of several thousands. It is not uncommon to turn over a rock and see hundreds of red mites running for shelter. Recently one scientist working in the far south of the Peninsula even found them living deep in a crack in a rock he had broken open. Excluding the sub-Antarctic, the region is home to about 70 mite species but only a few are free living. These include the hard-shelled mites that must be among the toughest terrestrial animals in the world. One species was found somehow surviving on a remote nunatak at 85 degrees South. The rest of the mites live on other animals such as the feather mites found on most Antarctic birds and the mites inhabiting the nasal passages of seals.

The springtails are iridescent black wingless insects which get their name from their prodigious jumping ability. They are the invertebrates that most people notice when visiting Antarctica because they occur in huge numbers and, by local standards, are large, growing up to 2 millimetres in length. Springtails have been found in all of Antarctica's ice-free habitats, and are the only free-living insects that survive on the harsher, main part of the continent. They are particularly common round penguin colonies where they make up 90 percent of all the insects and mites. Like some of the mites, springtails can be very gregarious and the females often come together to lay their eggs. They have no set breeding season, instead reproducing whenever the temperature rises above freezing. This is an essential adaptation for success in a very harsh environment. Springtails are also very long lived for invertebrates. Longevity is a common characteristic of Antarctic animals, allowing them another chance to breed if they lose the race in one year.

The mites and springtails have developed a number of techniques for surviving in the extreme cold. If they actually freeze, they will die, but they have the ability to supercool their bodies to below minus 30 degrees centigrade without ice crystals forming and some can even survive down to minus 50 degrees centigrade. Essential for this is the production of glycerol which acts as an antifreeze. During cold periods, they also starve themselves and empty their guts because the presence of minute fragments of food in the gut encourages the deadly ice crystals to form. While overwintering they may become completely encased in ice and quickly run out of oxygen as they respire. However they seem to have the ability to survive for up to a month without any oxygen at all. In addition, like many Antarctic invertebrates, they maintain especially high metabolic rates even at very low temperatures. This allows them to keep active in conditions that would make their temperate relatives unable to function.

The insect species over the whole of the continent and the maritime Antarctic total just 67 and of these, just 22 are free living. The rest are fleas or lice that live on seals or birds. These include the largest flea in the world, which is found on Antarctic fulmars and petrels. By carrying this unwanted passenger to their nests deep in the continent, the birds make it Antarctica's only flea. The largest permanent inhabitant of the continent is a 12 millimetre-long wingless midge called *Belgica antarctica*. It over-winters as a larva which, unlike those of the mites and springtails, is able to withstand freezing down to a temperature of minus 15 degrees centigrade. As always, the milder sub-Antarctic islands are richer. South Georgia boasts a single parasitic wasp and even harbours the world's most southerly spiders.

By the end of February, the warming effect of the sun and the erosive power of the waves have broken up the winter sea ice as far as it will go. The extent of the retreat varies from year to year depending on the weather conditions. Attached to the continent

A seal leaves its mark on an ice floe.

ABOVE *Freshly broken pack ice in Marguerite Bay. The further south you travel the thicker the pack becomes, until it is practically impenetrable.*

LEFT *A crabeater seal rests on an ice floe. Despite their name, crabeaters feed almost exclusively on krill.*

itself is an area of fast ice that never melts. Between its outer edge and the open ocean lies an often extensive area of broken ice known as pack ice, or the pack. This mixture of open water and ice is extremely mobile. Near the fast ice edge, the pack consists of massive slabs of ice, which are often kilometres across, but nearer to the ocean edge, it is a porridge of increasingly smaller pieces. The occasional iceberg floats along like a tall sailing ship on this semi-frozen sea.

The pack is an area of great beauty, partly because of the variety in shape and colour of the ice. Even in the harshest daylight, ice is not simply white. Depending on exactly how it was formed, the ice may be any shade of blue you can imagine to the brightest green of jade. As the sun sinks low in the southern sky, the pack may be touched with candy floss pink and under the light of the midnight sun, the wonderfully eroded shapes catch fire with oranges and reds. Such sights have been seen by very few because the pack is also an area of great unpredictability. If the wind changes direction, pack ice that was loosely spread will squeeze up tightly together and virtually open ocean can become solid ice within hours. Sir Ernest Shackleton experienced this while travelling in *Endurance* in 1915. In an attempt to minimize the length of his proposed journey right across the continent, Shackleton tried to sail as far south as he could into the pack ice of the Weddell Sea. He thought of the pack as a giant natural jigsaw puzzle and carefully picked his way through the pieces. Then the pack closed in, trapping *Endurance* and eventually crushing and sinking it.

For many years the dangers of the pack kept it an area of great mystery. But recently powerful modern icebreakers have allowed people to penetrate more deeply and the pack is revealing itself to be a very important Antarctic habitat. It is the only home of the second most numerous large mammal on Earth after humans. With a population of 14–30 million, the crabeater seal outnumbers the planet's other 32 or so species of seal put together, and its biomass is four times greater than all other seals. If its present rate of growth continues, there will be around 50 million crabeaters by the year 2000.

Despite their enormous population, it is rare to see more than 10 or 20 crabeaters together. They spend all their lives either in the sea or hauled out on icefloes in the pack, virtually never coming on to dry land. They are among the larger Antarctic seals, weighing about 220 kilograms, and are very attractive animals with a slim, streamlined body and a pointed nose. Their coat is coloured from silver to cream and a light flecking pattern adorns the shoulders, sides and, in some cases, the belly. Many individuals also bear deep scars inflicted by predatory leopard seals or killer whales which try to pull the crabeaters off icefloes.

Unlike the fur and elephant seals, crabeaters are fairly solitary animals and tend to breed in isolated pairs. The males do not need to be big, since they do not compete for a harem, and there is little difference in size between the sexes. If anything, the female tends to be a little larger than the male because she continues growing for longer. Crabeaters usually haul out on to the edge of the pack when they start breeding in September. They choose smaller floes with ridges or bumps that provide some sort of protection from the bad weather. A male will then defend his single female, vigorously maintaining a territory of radius 50 metres. Otherwise, though, crabeaters show little social organization.

A breeding group of crabeaters together on an icefloe give an image of close family life but this is misleading. After giving birth the mother suckles her pup for about four weeks. In this period the pup grows from about 20 kilograms to a weaning weight of about 110 kilograms, and sheds the thick fur it was born with for the shorter adult coat. During the same period the female does not eat at all and loses half of her body weight. Once she has weaned her pup, the female comes into oestrus and the male's advances become more and more determined. A very rough courtship follows in which the male repeatedly bites the female on her back and neck, and she may end up covered in her own blood. Once he is successful the male goes off to look for another female about to come into oestrus, leaving the female and pup on their own.

The vastness of the crabeater population can only really be appreciated from an aeroplane. Particularly in the spring, it is possible to fly for hour after hour over seemingly endless pack ice and continually spot the little black slugs of hauled out crabeaters. They are circumpolar and, though they only breed in the Antarctic, they are great wanderers. Every year vagrant crabeaters turn up at the tip of South America and round the Cape of South Africa. Their diet consists almost entirely of krill, each seal consuming about 20 kilograms a day. Their teeth are specially adapted to strain these crustaceans from the ocean. The premolars and molars, longer than normal, overlap to create a sieve and a special bony knob behind the last molar stops krill escaping through the gap. The seals catch their prey by swimming through swarms and snapping up individual krill or taking in a mouthful. The steady increase in crabeater numbers, like that of the fur seals, is probably related to the improved availability of krill since whaling devastated the other great krill consumers.

Relatively few birds spend much time in the pack. Sometimes the tiny black dots of Adélie penguins can be seen hitching a ride on an icefloe often many kilometres from their nearest nesting colony. Antarctic petrels and Wilson's storm petrels frequently venture into the pack and feed in the scattered openings in the ice. Much more common

PREVIOUS PAGE *Shelf ice off King George VI Sound is turned pink by the evening sun.*

A crabeater seal perfectly at ease under its natural home — the pack ice.

is the exquisite all-white snow petrel which seems more at home in Antarctica than almost any other animal.

The pack does have one more secret, an animal that is more elusive than any other south of the Polar Front. Living only in the very deepest pack, this animal was seen less than 50 times in the century after its discovery by Sir James Clark Ross. Even by the 1970s it had been observed by less than 100 people. Only the advent of powerful modern icebreakers has allowed people to travel regularly into the private world of the Ross seal. Nobody is sure of its exact numbers but recent estimates put the population at between 50 000 and 150 000, making it the Antarctic's rarest seal. It is a relatively small seal with an extraordinarily short snout, a wide head and very large eyes. Though Ross seals occur all round the continent, they are only found in the heart of the pack, south of 60 degrees, where they are thought to feed mainly on squid. Because they are so rarely seen very little is known about their breeding habits. But inevitably, like the crabeaters, they must fatten their young sufficiently for the pups to withstand the bitter cold of winter before the sun returns to the northern hemisphere and the ice closes in.

CHAPTER SIX

THE DOOR
CLOSES

The only thing which is certain about an Antarctic summer is that it will be very short. Particularly in the deep south, the sun's visit is all too brief and no sooner has the ice retreated to its minimum extent than it starts expanding again. Temperatures begin to drop, snow storms cover the bare rock and the ocean becomes increasingly restless. The door is closing and the pressure is on to finish breeding. In the penguin colonies, there are noticeable changes almost daily. As the chicks get larger, the ground of their colonies gradually turns pink, stained with spilt krill and penguin droppings. During the day the colony may be almost empty of adult birds because both parents are having to go to sea to satisfy their growing chicks. The chicks themselves gather together in creches, informal huddles that offer some protection from the autumn storms.

The larger colonies contain many thousands of chicks clustered in tight little groups and it seems remarkable that the returning parents can find their particular offspring among all the confusion. Chicks join creches very near their nests so it is probably easy for the parents to return to approximately the right area. But then they have to ensure that they feed only their young and they have developed a clever system for doing this. On arrival back at the creche, an adult calls to its chicks which immediately recognize the parent. Frantic for food, the chicks cajole the adult to regurgitate but, having caught its offspring's attention, the parent runs away from the creche. This is the start of a madcap chase for food that can take the chicks hundreds

Two full-grown Adélie penguin chicks enjoy the last of the autumn sun.

of metres across the colony and may last several minutes. While walking penguins look amusing enough to human eyes, penguins trying to move across the ground at speed are hysterically funny, particularly the chicks which call ceaselessly and are always tripping over. Eventually, in a quiet, open spot, the adult stops and feeds the hungry chicks. It was thought that these food chases allowed the parents to feed their offspring in peace away from other hungry chicks which might steal the precious krill. But studies of chinstrap penguins have shown that food chases occur more often and are longer when there are two chicks to feed rather than one. The hungriest of the chicks tends to be more persistent and usually wins the chase for food. So food chases also seem to be a good way for parents to regulate the distribution of food to their chicks.

As well as providing protection from bad weather, penguin creches are a defence against predators. Various animals depend heavily on penguins for food, one of the most persistent and certainly the strangest of which is the greater sheathbill. All white and about the size of a small crow, this bird gets its name from a horny sheath that covers its short pink bill, at the base of which are some fleshy protuberances. Nobody except another sheathbill could describe it as attractive. Its habits are also far from endearing for sheathbills are the Antarctic dustmen. Penguin faeces form an important part of their diet and anything that dies will quickly attract their attentions. They are bold, inquisitive and confident birds which strut around a colony looking for any opportunity to steal a meal. Early in the season they concentrate particularly on penguin eggs and will bang away with their bill at any egg left unattended for even a moment to get at the yolk. Many of the smaller first eggs laid by macaroni penguins become sheathbill dinners. They have even been known to burrow under incubating shags and steal the eggs of the unsuspecting adult. Once the penguin eggs have hatched, the sheathbills switch to stealing the chicks' dinners. When a penguin returns with krill for its chicks, the sheathbills will do anything to intercept the passage of food from beak to beak. Flying between the birds, they may actually land on a chick's back and grab the krill as it drops.

Greater sheathbills are found on South Georgia, the islands of the Scotia Arc and the Peninsula as far as 65 degrees South. They do not occur in large numbers but practically every colony of penguins or shags has its resident sheathbills. They time their breeding season to coincide with that of the penguins so that they are feeding their chicks just when the most krill is being brought back to the colony. As one might expect from the Antarctic's dustmen, sheathbill nests are rubbish tips. The nesting chamber is a burrow in heaps of shag guano or a crevice in some rocks, lined with scruffy bits of carcass, feather or bone. They lay two or three eggs but usually only one chick survives, suggesting that sheathbills may be cannibals on their own eggs or chicks. Despite all their nasty habits, these birds have to be respected for managing to exist on the fringes of the Antarctic food chain. They are the only truly terrestrial birds found in Antarctica, unable to survive without other animals on land to feed off, and must scrape a living through versatility. Many of those along the Peninsula stay throughout the winter when temperatures may fall to below minus 40 degrees centigrade. Others make remarkable journeys for birds with such apparently unsuitable wings, even venturing as far as South America.

If the Antarctic's dustmen are sheathbills, then its vultures must be the giant petrels. Even uglier to human eyes than the sheathbills, they are the largest of the petrels, about the size of a vulture with a 2 metre wingspan, and have a powerful hooked beak. The early whalers called them 'stinkers', 'stinkpots' or 'gluttons' and they continue to have a bad name. Though they are not just scavengers, relying on krill for up to a quarter of their diet, giant petrels are famous for their aggressive, rapacious behaviour. They will eat practically anything and are not afraid to fight for what they want. Their stomach contents have included squid, young shags, seaweed, penguins, the guts of seals and rope. There are even stories of giant petrels feeding on the bodies of sailors lost overboard. These birds often hang around penguin creches looking for a weak or isolated chick. Grabbing a flipper or a foot, they pull a squawking chick from the huddle and kill it with their powerful beak. Immediately the frightened members of the creche squeeze up tightly together, desperate not to be taken next.

There are two species of giant petrels. The northern giant petrel breeds only on the sub-Antarctic islands where it overlaps with the southern giant petrel. But the range of the southern species extends further down and all round the continent. It is one of the eight flying birds that breed in the harsh main part of the continent as well as the milder Peninsula. It could not survive there on krill alone and its existence relies on its ability to live off others, particularly penguin colonies and dead seals. While the sheathbills make a living by cunning, petrels rely on brute force and determination. Another bird has combined all these attributes to become one of the Antarctic's master tricksters and the most southerly occurring bird in the world. The Antarctic skua is regularly seen several hundreds of kilometres inland on the continent and has even turned up for short stays at the South Pole.

Despite their fearsome reputation, skuas are widely admired for their skill in the air and bold, confident appearance. The Antarctic has two skua species, both of which are heavy, broad-winged birds, about the size of a large gull with a fiercely hooked beak. The Antarctic skua's remarkable breeding range includes all round the continent and the Peninsula, and extends further south than any other flying bird. The slightly larger sub-Antarctic or brown skua lives further to the north and breeds on the maritime and sub-Antarctic islands. The southern extension of its range also includes the Antarctic Peninsula where the two species overlap. Both tend to be brownish birds with flashes of white feathers in their wings but they have a number of colour phases. The dark ground softens to a very light grey with age and during the breeding season, their necks are adorned with beautiful flecks of golden feathers.

Both skuas are superb on the wing, able to outfly and outmanoeuvre most other birds. These pirates of the air are famous for their habit of relentlessly pursuing other birds until they are forced to regurgitate the food in their crops. The chases are often spectacular with skua and victim twisting and turning in the air for many minutes. Even expert fliers in their own right, such as the terns and gulls, find it very difficult to throw off a determined skua. Sometimes the victim will fly straight into the sea, hoping its persecutor will give up. Skuas also have a taste for the eggs and chicks of other birds. A single pair has wiped out complete colonies of nesting Antarctic terns and penguin colonies always have their attendant skuas on the look out for a quick meal.

The two skua species have rather different foraging techniques. Though the Antarctic skua will steal eggs and chicks, it spends most of its time catching food at sea. Early in the breeding season it concentrates on krill and only later does it turn to fish, penguin eggs and chicks. In one study at the Adélie penguin colony at Cape Bird in the deep south of the Ross Sea, there were 250 pairs of Antarctic skuas breeding round 24 000 pairs of Adélies. It was estimated that the skuas stole 23 000 penguin eggs during the course of one season, but fish, krill and squid were their main foods. Sub-Antarctic skuas, on the other hand, spend very little time foraging at sea and are far more dependent on other birds for their food. They will attack almost any Antarctic bird but penguins are the main focus of their interest and so they tend to nest near them. The skuas then hang over the penguin colony throughout the breeding season like the black shadow of death.

Strutting quietly among a colony, a skua will suddenly stab its powerful beak underneath an incubating penguin to get at its eggs. Often two skuas co-operate in schemes to rob the penguins of their eggs or chicks. For example, one may grab the tail of a penguin and pull it off its nest while another steals the eggs. Meanwhile air-borne skuas are almost continually cruising at low level, looking for a chance to snatch an egg or chick. Later, when parent penguins are spending much of their time foraging for their chicks, they return from trips to face harassment from skuas intent on stealing their krill. It is a constant battle with the brave penguins chasing off skuas on the ground

ABOVE *The chick of an Antarctic skua shelters under its parent's wing. This bird is nesting in the extensive banks of moss that manage to grow in the milder conditions found along the Antarctic Peninsula.*

RIGHT *A giant petrel steals a terrified chick from a creche of young Adélies. The petrel has chosen a smaller, weaker bird that has still to moult its down.*

A pair of sub-Antarctic skuas perform an ear-splitting and long call. This display serves to mark their territory and warn off any rivals.

only to find others threatening from above. The chicks huddled in their creches have the advantage of numbers but often the clever skuas find a way to get at one. They may swoop down to distract the adults one minute and then the next, fly straight at the chicks, grab one by the head and carry it struggling away.

Though happy to steal other birds' chicks, skuas are very careful to defend their own offspring. They are quite social nesters, making simple scrap nests within 50 metres of each other. They are also very territorial and, particularly when they have eggs or chicks, defend their patch with great vigour. Other birds are warned off by the so-called long call, which is also sometimes used when a pair of skuas greet each other. Holding both wings up behind it so that it looks like a Viking helmet, the skua throws up its head and gives a loud long call that echoes through the Antarctic quiet. If this vocal warning is not enough to deter an intruder, the skua takes to the air and protects its chicks with frantic dive-bombing, apparently unafraid of hitting the intruder with legs or beak. Any person accidentally walking near a skua's nest may suddenly hear a loud rush of wings as over 2–3 kilograms of bird comes racing past an ear. Since skua attacks often draw blood, an island covered in their nests is well worth avoiding.

The timing of a skua's breeding is very dependent on its food. The sub-Antarctic skuas tend to time their egg laying so that their chicks will hatch at the same time as those of the penguins. Antarctic skuas lay about two weeks later and their breeding success is strongly linked to the availability of krill and fish. In years when the sea ice is slow to break up, the Antarctic skuas have more difficulty foraging at sea and their clutches often fail. Sub-Antarctic skuas do not face this seasonal problem and their breeding is generally successful year after year. On the Peninsula, where the species overlap, sub-Antarctic skuas are outnumbered eight to one by Antarctic skuas but still tend to exclude them from the penguin colonies. Sometimes individuals from the two species pair up and breed. Interestingly, both birds in such hybrid pairs continue using the foraging technique typical of their species. Unlike the sheathbills, shags and giant petrels, which remain throughout the winter, all the skuas fly north in May. Ringing has shown that during the southern winter they undertake a great clockwise journey round the whole of Antarctica, penetrating far to the north. Birds have been recovered in California and even Britain and northern Japan.

As the middle of February approaches, the Adélie chicks that have survived attack by the vultures and the pirates must prepare to depart the colony and head to sea. The days are growing shorter, autumn storms are becoming more frequent and the temperature is beginning to drop. Before long the sea will start to freeze again and any chicks that have not left the colony will be trapped. The Adélies are under greater

At the end of the season, creches of Adélie penguin chicks are pink with spilt krill and droppings.

pressure than other penguin chicks because their nest sites in the deep south will become ice locked first. Adélie chicks develop quickly, taking just over 50 to 60 days from hatching to fledging. Gentoo chicks take between 70 and 90 days and so no gentoo penguin can breed further south than 65 degrees. If it did, its chicks would not be ready to leave before the sea ice reformed and cut off their vital access to the ocean.

Before they can enter the sea, the Adélie chicks must shed the coat of fluffy down that has insulated them through the summer. This comes off in chunks and some half-moulted chicks waddle round looking like the last of the Mohicans, with a crest of down left on their heads. Over a two-week period the creches break up as parents try to lead their chicks to the beach. Increasingly, parents only feed their offspring by the sea and the number of chicks there gradually builds up, all gathering confidence for their first leap. Just as flying birds are nervous of their first flight, so penguin chicks are clearly wary of the water. When they do venture in, they are still too buoyant to swim or dive well and tens of them splash round on the surface looking like wind-up bathroom toys. Eventually, though, they start diving under water and discovering the medium they were designed for. Then the parents have to get on with their own moult and they abandon any late chicks. Even the more mature chicks are still thin birds, only 70 percent of their adult weight. On their own, with no more help from their parents, they must grow and fatten quickly during the last days of summer. Those that succeed head north to spend the next two or three years in the Southern Ocean. In just a couple of weeks, an area that was covered with a noisy confusion of breeding penguins can become completely deserted.

The Adélie chicks' first timid dips in the sea do not go unnoticed. One Antarctic predator lies in wait under the waves knowing that the fledging chicks will provide a bounty. The leopard seal, with an estimated population of just under a quarter of a million, is probably the Antarctic's most fearsome seal. This large but slim animal has a snake-like neck, a triangular head and a mouth that seems permanently fixed in an evil grin but opens sometimes to reveal a sharp set of teeth. It gets its name from the spots that pattern its belly and its solitary hunting habits. Also like its namesake, the leopard seal relies on stealth and surprise to catch its prey. As the time approaches for the penguin chicks to enter the water, leopard seals start to gather in the waters round the colonies. They keep themselves well hidden and only occasionally do their reptilian heads appear above the surface. Certainly the chicks learning to swim seem blissfully unaware of the threat until a seal suddenly surges out of the water and grabs one of them. The chicks are easy prey because, being poor divers, they have little chance of escape. Like a cat with a mouse, the seal often plays with its victim for 10 minutes or

ABOVE *Adélie penguin chicks gather on the beaches of their breeding island preparing to take their first-ever swim. An adult Adélie leaps in first to show them what to do.*

RIGHT *A leopard seal violently thrashes the body of an Adélie penguin chick against the surface of the water. This process strips little pieces of meat off the carcass. The seal may spend up to an hour slowly eating the chick in this way.*

more rather than killing it straight away. Time after time the chick lying motionless and apparently dead in the seal's mouth is released and swims away only to be chased and caught again. Finally, with a powerful, lethal flick of its head, the seal smashes the chick on the surface of the water. Even then the seal continues to thrash the chick's body against the sea for the next hour or so, stripping off the feathers. Throughout the violent process, the seal nibbles little scraps of flesh until only the penguin's bones and skin remain. Intact and inside out, the skin sinks to the bottom like a discarded jacket.

Leopard seals do not prey on the chicks alone. Early in the season, when Adélie penguins are walking across the still-frozen sea to their colonies, leopard seals follow underneath and suddenly smash up through the ice to grab a meal. Later on, when the ice has melted, the seals patrol the waters near the colonies waiting for the adult Adélies as they come and go on foraging trips. This has a dramatic effect on the birds, which is particularly noticeable on their return. Instead of coming gently ashore, they swim in at great speed. Then, although flightless, they take to the air, throwing themselves out of the water in a desperate attempt to avoid a seal's snatching jaws. The adults that are caught get the same thrashing treatment as their chicks and the sea becomes red with penguin blood. In an Adélie colony containing 200 000 nesting pairs, some leopard seals took 4800 adults and 1200 chicks in one year. This was a lot of food for a small number of leopard seals but for the colony it represented just over 1 percent of the chicks.

Leopard seals have a catholic taste which includes other seals. Over 80 percent of crabeater seals bear scars inflicted by leopard seals, suggesting that attacks are regular and largely unsuccessful. In fact, leopard seals are successful in taking young crabeater pups, up to about 5 months old, but older pups generally escape with just a few scars. It is thought that male leopard seals are the main hunters, particularly when the females are tending their pups. In the winter, and when penguins and seals are not available, leopard seals will also feed off squid, fish and krill. About 50 percent of their diet is krill and, like the crabeater seals, their teeth can neatly overlap to form a sieve for straining the crustaceans from the sea. Again like the crabeaters, leopard seals live mainly along the edge of the pack although they do go north to visit the sub-Antarctic islands.

By the time February comes to a close, the adult Adélies have left their chicks but have one more important task to complete before the sea ice drives them north again. They must moult their feathers and replace them with a new set to protect them during their winter at sea. Moulting is a very energy-consuming process and, before it can begin, the adults must regain the weight they lost while rearing their chicks. So they go to sea to feed for about three weeks and then return to their nesting colonies.

Moulting chinstrap penguins cover the slopes of Deception Island with a blizzard of feathers.

SEASONAL CHANGES IN SEA ICE COVERAGE

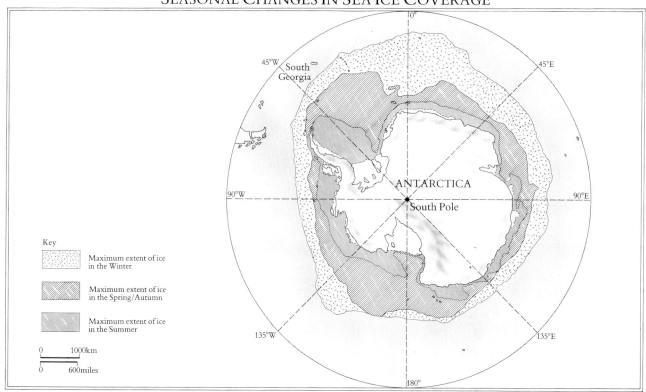

Key

Maximum extent of ice
in the Winter

Maximum extent of ice
in the Spring/Autumn

Maximum extent of ice
in the Summer

0   1000km

0   600miles

The difference between a congregation of breeding chinstraps and the later moulting penguins is so great that it seems as though another species has taken over the colony. Nesting chinstraps are extremely noisy, some of them always seem to be fighting and there is a constant flow of penguins on the move. When they return to moult, the penguins space themselves out across the ground, leaving exactly the same gap between each bird. None moves a muscle and for almost three weeks there is total silence. Slowly all the old feathers are shed and new ones grow through. Before long the colony looks as if a sudden snowstorm had coated the ground with white as millions of old feathers blow on the wind. During the complete moult the penguins lose 1.5 to 2 kilograms, which is nearly half their original body weight. The prize is a new set of feathers to help them survive the rigours of the Antarctic winter.

By the end of March practically all the penguins in the deep south have completed their moult and are heading north for the open ocean. In the months that follow the days will get shorter and shorter, and temperatures will continue to drop. Slowly, far more slowly than it broke up, the sea begins to freeze again. It starts with the formation of frazil ice, a slush made up of clumps of ice crystals. As these ice crystals condense to form a thick layer at the surface, the water takes on a dull matt appearance known as grease ice. In stable, calm conditions, the crystals can become stacked in long needles of congelation ice. The action of the waves shapes the ice into circular 'pancakes' with upturned edges. These jostle together in a jigsaw called pancake ice. Increasing mechanical stress and cold convert this spongy mass into hard ice. Ice crystals form on the bottom and, little by little, the thickness of the ice increases to several metres. It starts to form in the deep south and gradually advances north by just over 4 kilometres a day. Around the whole continent this represents an increase in area of ice of 100 000 square kilometres per day. The sea ice can develop even more quickly than this if pack ice, blown together by a storm, then freezes.

The formation of ice is a relentless process that maintains and gains its own momentum. Gradually the entire length of the Peninsula and all the maritime islands are trapped once more in ice. Almost all the larger animals – the birds, seals and whales – are driven north by its progress. The covering of ice also reduces the amount of sunlight penetrating to the sea. The sunlight is itself weakening as the sun is travelling north, and so the phytoplankton no longer blooms. Krill swarms disperse and the whole Southern Ocean food chain slows down. Snowstorms become more frequent, cloaking the bare rock of summer. Mosses and lichens, and the invertebrates they support, close down for the winter. In the south, the brief summer is over and the door has closed.

Female fur seals can return to suckle their pups because the sea round sub-Antarctic Islands rarely freezes.

LEFT *A South Georgia pintail scavenges scraps of meat from a fur seal carcass using a hole in the skin made for it by a giant petrel.*

BELOW *First into the freshly dead carcass of a young elephant seal, a giant petrel covers its head and powerful beak with blood. Skuas fly in for the second sitting.*

To the north, the sub-Antarctic islands usually escape the icy grip but the pressure to finish breeding is just as intense. Plummeting temperatures and worsening storms will kill any late young and the ocean is gradually becoming a harder place for the adults to find food in. By March the fur seals' breeding beaches, which only weeks before were crammed with fighting males, are all but deserted. They resemble a battlefield after a dreadful slaughter has taken place. Running with water and thick with mud, the ground is covered with the skins and skeletons of seals that lost the fight to reproduce. The males left at the end of December just after the battle had reached its peak, leaving the beach littered with the fresh carcasses of males that had been killed in territorial disputes and of pups that had been crushed in the scuffles. For the scavengers this slaughter provided a splendid feast.

The first down to a fresh carcass are always giant petrels. Their size and large powerful bills allow them to cut through the thick fur seal pelts. After plucking out the eyes, the petrels break a small hole through the skin. Within moments, their heads disappear into the body of the freshly dead seal to emerge dripping with bright red blood and with a long strand of intestine gripped firmly in the beak. There is constant squabbling as one petrel tries to assert dominance over another. The birds face up to each other, spreading their tails wide, holding their wings out and lowering threatening heads close to the ground. Despite such diversions, in just a few noisy hours a group of petrels will fight their way through a complete seal carcass.

Both the northern and southern giant petrels occur on the sub-Antarctic islands. They look very similar except that the southern species has a green tip to its bill while the northern species has a brown-tipped bill. Their diets are also broadly similar, both birds being principally scavengers and predators. On Bird Island, adult macaroni penguins injured or killed by seals make up over half the food giant petrels give to their chicks. All the burrowing petrels, except the larger white-chinned, fall victim to them. The female giant petrels spend most of their time at sea foraging for krill, fish and cephalopods. Male petrels are larger and stronger than their mates with more powerful bills and it is they that scavenge regularly on carcasses. However, only the northern giant petrels can take full advantage of the bounty of dead fur seals in December. The northern species nests earlier than its southern counterpart and its chicks are just hatching as the seal battles are underway, while the southern giant petrel is still incubating its eggs.

The giant petrels are not the only birds that take advantage of the seals' misfortune. After the petrels have made the first incision, sub-Antarctic skuas join in the fray. Sheathbills are quick to nip in between the legs of the larger birds and pick up any available scraps. On South Georgia, fur seal battlefields also receive a far more surprising visitor than these regular scavengers. The South Georgia pintail is a small brown duck with a bright yellow beak and, quite unlike any other member of its family, has a taste for mammal flesh. Its bill is totally unsuited to ripping skin but, once there is even the smallest hole in the carcass, the duck will get its head right inside. Unlike the messy petrels, the pintails are very fastidious and keep washing themselves clean in streams or ponds.

The South Georgia pintail is a charming bird that somehow seems out of place in the tough Antarctic environment. It is one of only two ducks that nest in the Antarctic, the other being the speckled teal. Both breed on South Georgia and they look so similar that for a long time people did not realize that the far less numerous speckled teal was there at all. There are thought to be only 40 to 50 pairs of teal nesting round just one bay. The whaling station at Grytviken is very close by and they were probably introduced by whalers. The speckled teal seems to prefer large areas of permanent fresh water and these are in short supply which probably stops its population expanding. While carcasses are a useful supplement to the far more widespread South Georgia pintail's diet, most of its food comes from the small freshwater ponds found around the island. Groups of four or five pintails are often seen on the ponds where they behave very much like other dabbling ducks. They are constantly upending in search of copepods and fairy shrimps, which are a favourite prey. The pintails nest among the tussock and pairs have a delightful courtship display. Both birds lift their chins up and down at each other and give a happy little 'burp-whistle' call that all visitors to South Georgia remember with affection.

Though the male fur seals depart in December almost immediately after copulation, the females and pups have to stay a lot longer. The Antarctic fur seal is the only fur seal to breed in the Antarctic and it takes longer to wean its young than any other fur seal, which probably reflects the demands of Antarctic life. The females continue to suckle their pups until late February or early March, by which time the waves beside the breeding beaches are thick with the endearing faces of young fur seals. In contrast, the beaches that resounded early in the summer with the roars of fighting elephant seals were quiet by the end of December. Female elephant seals wean their pups in just 27 days, and the males and females then quickly return to the sea to make up the weight they lost while breeding. However, the adult elephant seals must return to land again during the autumn to moult their coats. It is difficult to believe that a seal weighing several tonnes could become lost in a pool of mud but that is exactly what happens during the moulting period. The elephant seals go inland behind the beaches and churn

A grey-headed albatross chick on its nest awaiting the return of its parents with food.

out great wallows of mud and water, usually where a stream used to flow. Then they lie there, often with just the nostrils and the eyes poking through the thick soup of mud. Even these are obscured on cold days by the constant cloud of steam rising from the hollow. Gradually their old coat peels off in strips and by the end of May, the seals have finished their moult and can return to sea.

The penguins of the sub-Antarctic islands, like their more southerly breeding relatives, also need a new set of feathers for the winter. During early March the colonies of macaroni penguins empty for a week or so and then the adults return to moult. By mid to late April, the colonies are almost deserted again, the adults having gone off to spend the winter far out at sea leaving the rocky hillsides white with discarded feathers. The gentoo penguins follow a similar pattern, although many of these birds remain on their nesting beaches during the winter. The lack of winter ice gives the penguins of the north this freedom. It also allows the smaller albatrosses to feed their chicks until May when they fledge. Towards the end of autumn, their colonies are filled with fluffy chicks sitting bolt upright on upturned saucepan nests, waiting for their parents to return with food. Foraging is not always easy for the adults, and only about 50 percent of the offspring of grey-headed and sooty albatrosses survive. For black-browed albatrosses, relying on unpredictable krill supplies, the problem is particularly acute and, on average, only 36 percent of their chicks fly the nest.

As the sub-Antarctic islands seem to be closing down for the winter, some wandering albatrosses are still courting. Young birds that have as yet no mate gather in open areas in the tussock called greens. These areas need to be large to allow the birds to spread their 3.5 metre wingspan in display. Up to 13 younger wanderers have been seen together but usually a green contains just one or two males and the female they are trying to impress. Their courtship is often called the ecstatic display because that is exactly how the birds appear. Spreading their massive wings, they shake their heads at each other, whining all the time. Then, starting to vibrate the mandibles of its enormous beak, each bird gradually raises its head up to the sky and closes the bill with a loud snap as it reaches the vertical. This goes on for some time interspersed, often when another albatross is flying over, with the bird throwing its head up into the air and making sky calls. Eventually, with bills pointed vertically, the birds emit a powerful braying whistle followed by an inhaled sigh. This courtship ritual is one of the most impressive of any bird and it needs to be because the wanderers form permanent partnerships. On South Georgia, the young birds take two or three years to establish a bond with their lifelong mates and their displays are a spectacular climax to the busy Antarctic summer.

With the sun's departure the Antarctic effectively closes down for another long winter.

CHAPTER SEVEN

THE
BIG FREEZE

O<small>N</small> 27 J<small>UNE</small> 1911, three men left the comfort of Captain Scott's hut at Cape Evans in the Ross Sea to undertake a 97 kilometre journey to the emperor penguin colony at Cape Crozier. They left at eleven o'clock in the morning in pitch darkness and, though there was not a breath of wind blowing, the temperature was already down to minus 26 degrees centigrade. It was the first time that anybody had attempted to travel through the depths of the Antarctic winter. Just five days earlier, Edward Wilson, 'Birdie' Bowers and Apsley Cherry-Garrard had spent midwinter's day with the rest of Scott's party. This is the most important day in the Antarctic calendar, celebrating the sun reaching its most northerly position and starting the slow return south again.

It was Edward Wilson who had persuaded Scott to allow them to undertake a journey that everyone knew carried with it enormous risks. Ten years earlier, both men had been on the *Discovery* when the very first emperor penguin colony was found off Cape Crozier. It was October 1902, early in the Antarctic spring, when they saw a group of emperor chicks out on the ice and Wilson was fascinated that any bird could have such well-grown young so early in the season. The only explanation he could think of was that the emperors were laying their eggs on ice in the depths of winter. This seemed incredible but Wilson was determined to find out whether his idea was correct by visiting a breeding colony during the long polar night.

For 19 days of permanent night, the three men dragged two sledges, which together weighed a third of a tonne, over a dreadfully crevassed ice sheet. The temperature dropped to minus 61 degrees centigrade, their clothes and harnesses froze solid and all of them suffered terrible frostbite. Time after time, vicious gales suddenly blew in across the ice sheet, forcing the men to stay for days in their tiny tent.

Emperor penguins overwinter in Antarctica and endure the world's worst weather conditions.

*In winter, temperatures in
Antarctica drop as low as minus
70 degrees centigrade.*

Cherry-Garrard wrote of those storms, 'Ten minutes and it was blowing as though the world was having a fit of hysterics'. Despite hallucinating through lack of sleep and continual straining in the dark, they did eventually reach Cape Crozier and found, as Wilson had hoped, a group of emperor penguins huddled on the ice, incubating their eggs. 'After indescribable effort and hardship we were witnessing a marvel of the natural world, and we were the first and only men who had ever done so'.

The fact that Cherry-Garrard survived to write those words was also something of a marvel. The morning after the men had successfully collected three precious emperor penguin eggs, a hurricane ripped their camp apart. It blew for several days, stealing away the tent and destroying the canvas roof of their simple stone shelter: 'The earth was torn in pieces; the indescribable fury and roar of it all cannot be imagined.' Left with no shelter other than their sleeping bags, they huddled together like the emperors, desperate to share body warmth. They were very lucky that the storm soon abated and even luckier to find their tent undamaged. When they finally staggered into the hut at Cape Evans they were looked upon as 'beings from another world'. In Scott's words they had achieved 'the hardest journey ever made'.

Even today, people treat the Antarctic winter with great respect. For six months much of the continent is thrown into almost complete darkness. High up on the icecap, temperatures drop to below minus 70 degrees centigrade. From there, the world's most powerful winds rush down to further chill a continental coastline that is separated from the open ocean by several hundred kilometres of sea ice. While Edward Wilson and his companions were extremely fortunate to survive just a few nights exposed to the long Antarctic night, the male emperor penguins spend nearly four months on the ice without a single meal. They are the most impressive members of a very select group of creatures that cheat the Antarctic winter. One penguin, a solitary seal, a few tiny insects and a handful of simple plants make up the list of Antarctica's permanent residents, the survivors in a wilderness that demands more from those that exist there than any other place on Earth. Apart from temporary human residents, the only mammal that remains in the deep south throughout the winter is the Weddell seal.

Weddells breed further south than any other mammal on Earth. While Ross and crabeater seals choose the pack ice region further to the north, Weddells have opted for the permanent fast ice that never breaks up even in summer. Part of the population moves north to the pack ice during the winter, but many Weddell seals remain in the south throughout the year. This remarkable achievement is only possible because the seals have found a way to get year-round access to the sea. Without this they would have no source of food and, anyway, would be unable to survive for long out on the ice with temperatures down to minus 50 degrees centigrade. They manage to spend the months of winter darkness almost permanently in the water by maintaining holes in the fast ice through which they can breathe. Few who have seen it fail to marvel at the extraordinary sight of a Weddell seal's head peeping out in the darkness from a hole in fast ice many metres thick, but its survival in the deep south has a cost. Weddells are equipped with protruding canine and incisor teeth which they use to literally grind down the ice around their holes. If they fail to do so, even for a short time, the holes will freeze over and the seals will drown. The relentless task gradually wears down their teeth and eventual tooth loss is probably the reason why few Weddell seals reach 20 years of age, while crabeaters are known to live for almost twice as long.

For many people, the Weddell is the most beautiful of all the Antarctic seals. It is a big animal, 3 metres long and weighing 400–500 kilograms in spring, with a grey coat covered in a superb pattern of black spots. Its head is relatively small and it has a friendly, almost smiling face. The total population is stable and estimated at about 800 000 animals, most of which live year round in the fast ice. During the winter there is something of a northerly migration and the adolescent animals tend to be kept out of the southern breeding areas by older males. Weddell seals prefer areas in the fast ice where pressure has folded the ice into hummocks and bumps. The cracks which tend to form in this rough ice help provide the seals with a good supply of holes. Flying over the sea ice during early spring, all you can see is endless white broken just here and there by seal holes, like oases in the desert.

The females start to haul themselves out for breeding at the beginning of spring, which comes in September at the edge of the fast ice and November further south. The Weddell's breeding system is an unusual one for a mammal and an interesting halfway stage between the solitary coupling of leopard and crabeater seals and the polygynous fur and elephant seals in which each male defends a harem of many females. The male Weddell is slightly smaller than the female, suggesting that he does not attempt to claim a number of females. However, the Weddell is polygynous, although the male is lucky to get 10 females rather than up to 100 like some elephant seal bulls. Each male Weddell defends a three-dimensional underwater territory surrounding a hole in the ice. All the females that come and go from that hole to have their pups will mate with that one male.

The males have to fight hard to keep their territories, which diminish in area from 6000 square metres early in the season to half that as pressure for females increases. Because their fights occur under water few have been observed but many males bear scars as evidence. They are often particularly badly damaged around the genital region,

ABOVE *Weddell seal pups are born straight onto the sea ice and are suddenly ejected from a womb at plus 37 degrees centigrade into a world that may well be below minus 30.*

LEFT *Unless Weddell seals can keep open their breathing holes in the ice throughout the winter, they cannot survive. They use their teeth to grind away the fresh ice that is constantly forming.*

so the battles may involve one male chasing another and trying to bite at its genital slit. Unless they are basking on the ice, nursing wounds inflicted in battles they lost below, the males spend almost all their time under water. About half of them hold territories while the others are just transients passing through. Only about half of the females breed each year too, the other half forgoing the opportunity possibly because suitable breeding holes are in short supply.

The females have their pups almost as soon as they haul out. Since they do this early in the spring, the births must be a great shock for the pups. The young leave a womb at 37 degrees centigrade and within seconds find themselves lying on ice at minus 20 degrees centigrade. The pups are about 25 kilograms at birth and covered with soft grey down. Their mother's milk is one of the richest known, containing 60 percent fat, and the pups double their weight in just 18 days. They also lose the down for a beautiful coat of silver-grey fur which must protect them during dreadful storms that cover them with snow and seem to almost freeze up their tiny faces. Their mothers are anxious to persuade them to seek shelter under the ice as soon as possible. The pups make their first brave venture under water when they are only seven to ten days old. They are weaned at about seven weeks old, when they weigh just over 110 kilograms, and are completely independent after just two or three months. Meanwhile the females come into oestrus soon after giving birth, and mate under water staying near the hole in the ice.

The life of the Weddell is split into two very distinct halves by a few metres of fast ice. Above the ice, the seals face some of the harshest conditions on Earth with temperatures continually well below freezing, total darkness for months and the strongest of winds. Their world under the ice is a much more peaceful place where winds are unknown and it is never colder than minus 1.8 degrees centigrade. Even in summer, little sunlight penetrates the ice and the seals live in an eerie gloom, communicating with each other in a series of weird, lonely calls that bounce off the ice and carry for kilometres under water. On the surface they are lumbering lumps of blubber but under water they are the masters of their element, the supreme divers among the seals. Weddells perform long shallow dives which can last from 20 to 73 minutes and take them as far as 12 kilometres from their original hole. During these exploratory dives, the seals always have the ice within their sight and they probably use shallow dives to find new breathing holes.

Although Weddells may eat a range of invertebrates, including squid and octopus, their diet consists mainly of fish. They are particularly fond of Antarctic cod, large deep-water fish, and they will go down to 740 metres or deeper to catch them.

Most feeding dives are between 200 and 400 metres and tend to be short, lasting just 5 to 25 minutes. These deep dives are remarkable for a mammal because most mammals would at least suffer 'the bends' after diving to such depths. This problem develops when the great pressure of water at depth forces nitrogen present in the air of the lungs into the bloodstream. As the diver rises to the surface and the pressure reduces, bubbles of nitrogen are released in the body and cause 'the bends'. The seals avoid the problem by having a flexible rib cage which can collapse as pressure builds up, usually between 40 and 80 metres down. The collapse gets rid of the nitrogen but also leaves the seal with little oxygen. To cope with this, the heart rate slows down and blood circulation to the seal's muscles and extremities is restricted, concentrating scarce oxygen at the brain, heart and lungs.

It is not just Weddell seals that benefit from the protection provided by several metres of fast ice. The waters covered by permanent ice are a stable, predictable environment which changes little through the year. They are a haven where a number of animals can withstand the worst of the winter. When krill swarms break up at the end of summer, it is thought that many of these crustaceans end up living under the ice for the winter months. There they can feed on the algae that grows slowly practically all year round inside the ice itself. Enormous numbers of other crustaceans, the amphipods, graze the bottom surface of the ice. Tiny fish shelter in cracks in the ice, their blood loaded with antifreeze to avoid lethal ice crystals forming in their bodies. And divers who have followed the Weddells down to the depths have discovered a seabed covered in a marvellous wealth of resident invertebrates.

The great enemy for life on the ocean bed, or benthic life, is ice. Nothing can survive the annual formation of sea ice or the powerful scraping of giant icebergs and scouring by pack ice. But below 30 metres, and particularly where fast ice protects the waters, the benthic life can be extremely rich. In fact, the seabed life in the Antarctic is twice as rich, diverse and dense as the better-known Arctic benthic fauna. In deeper Antarctic water, there is an incredible abundance of sponges. These are not the horny ones typical of tropical waters but exquisite glass sponges with an internal skeleton made from an intricate lattice of silicon spicules. Growing to over a metre high, they provide the trees in a beautiful invertebrate jungle. Sheltering beneath their canopy is a rich variety of amphipods, sea spiders, isopods and molluscs. Sometimes the whole seabed is covered with countless red starfish, while estimates of brittlestar numbers have reached 100 million in just 1 square kilometre.

Many of the seabed creatures are giants of their kind. An isopod, *Glyptonotus antarcticus,* grows up to 20 centimetres long, about three times bigger than most of its

THE ANTARCTIC CONTINENT

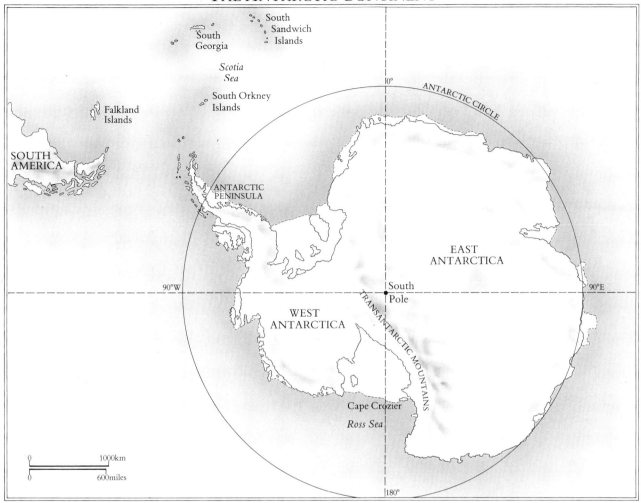

Starfish, sea squirts, algae and anemones cover a rock face which is protected from erosion by ice.

kind. It fills the niche occupied elsewhere by crabs, which are strangely missing from the Antarctic sea floor. There are also bright orange sea spiders with 10 or 12 giant legs, 5 centimetre amphipods, and oversized polychaetes, or rag worms, all specially adapted for life in cold water. The giant size of many of the Antarctic's bottom-living invertebrates is related to their slow growth. The cold temperatures and the low level of food available overall mean that life runs in slow motion. This, in turn, results in many animals living a very long time, including a starfish known to have reached at least 39 years old and a limpet that survived for a century. Not all Antarctic animals are giants, though. It is very difficult for animals that use a lot of calcium in their bodies to grow well in cold temperatures. While soft-bodied animals and silicon-based creatures such as glass sponges grow to enormous sizes, calcium-based animals such as the molluscs with shells end up as dwarves.

The cold of the Antarctic affects the life cycle of many of the animals living on the seabed. Generally they tend to produce fewer, larger eggs than their counterparts in warmer seas and to protect them with greater care. They often lay their eggs in the winter months so that the juveniles hatch in the spring and can benefit fully from the phytoplankton blooms. The cold also lowers the benthic animals' metabolic rates and so reduces their need for food, which is an advantage in an environment where food is in very short supply. Most of their sparse food drops as crumbs from the faster lifestyle going on above them. Many Antarctic invertebrates have become scavengers, feeding on anything that has died and sunk to the seabed, such as a penguin carcass. They also feed on anything discarded and seal faeces are the most important sources of food for invertebrates living under Weddell seal holes.

The most southerly Weddell seal population in Antarctica is that beside White Island in the Ross Sea. No other mammal breeds closer to the South Pole which is just under 1300 kilometres away. It is not an easy place to live. The island is completely surrounded by the Ross Ice Shelf and the seals must somehow dive down through ice over 70 metres thick. Even in summer, when the sea ice has broken up, White Island is still separated from open water by 22 kilometres of ice shelf. This distance is too far for any seal to swim without coming up for air and as a result, the White Island Weddell seals are completely stranded. Throughout their lives, they can only use the cracks immediately beside the island.

The White Island Weddells live in the shadow of another of the Antarctic's greatest survival stories – Mount Erebus. The highest active volcano on the continent, it is a perfect white cone above an expanse of flat sea ice. Captain Scott built his overwintering hut on its lower slopes so that the party returning from the pole could use the volcano to find their way home. They never had the chance but Erebus remains an important landmark. There, on the coldest continent on Earth, the warm heart of the planet makes its presence felt. The volcano's slopes are completely covered with glaciers but in its caldera, red hot lava bubbles away. On the mountain's summit, at 3974 metres, the altitude ensures that in the height of summer temperatures rarely rise above minus 20 degrees centigrade. Yet even the summit has been colonized by life. The heat from the volcano melts the ice just around the rim of the caldera and in that exposed rock highly specialized bacteria and algae somehow manage to scrape a living. Quite extraordinarily, for the Antarctic, these simple organisms are adapted to live in hot conditions.

The summit of Mount Erebus also offers an unparalleled view. To the north lies Cape Evans where Captain Scott's historic hut still stands, preserved by the cold almost exactly as he left it. A little further north at Cape Royds is the hut used by Shackleton when he overwintered, built right beside the most southerly penguin colony on the planet. A few thousand Adélies nest there knowing, as did the early explorers, that the sea ice will retreat no further south. Immediately below, the glacier tongue of Mount Erebus extends out into the permanent fast ice. And to the west, the distant horizon is filled by the Transantarctic Mountains, a welcome sight in a landscape so dominated by flat, featureless ice sheets.

The Transantarctic Mountains chain stretches more than 2200 kilometres across Antarctica. The continent is made up of two parts, East and West Antarctica, and tectonic activity along the boundary between them created the mountain chain. It is one of the most impressive in the world, with many peaks rising above 4000 metres, yet little of the chain is visible because it is almost entirely engulfed in ice. Along the Ross Sea near Mount Erebus, the Transantarctics just manage to keep back the great ice sheet of East Antarctica. But here and there the ice sheet does break through and some of the world's largest glaciers come tumbling down over 3000 metres from the icecap to the sea. Flying along the Transantarctic chain, the world seems locked in a permanent winter. In one direction the featureless icecap disappears uninterrupted to the pole, while in another there is just the flat expanse of endless sea ice. Down below, beautiful mountain peaks sharpened razor thin by frost are swallowed up by more ice. Yet hidden in the Transantarctics among all this white is the continent's largest single area of bare rock, the 3000 square kilometres of the Dry Valleys.

The Dry Valleys were discovered by a party from Captain Scott's expedition to the Ross Sea in 1901–4. Returning through the fog from a sledging trip on the icecap, the party tried to reach Cape Evans by following a glacier descending through the

mountains. Then the fog cleared and, to their surprise, they saw that the glacier stopped dead in a valley completely free of ice. Since they were equipped for travelling over ice by sledge this proved a great inconvenience, forcing them to retrace their steps. The valley that impeded them is one of three major Dry Valleys, none of which have had a covering of snow for millions of years. Any snow that falls soon ablates, going directly from ice to vapour and avoiding the liquid state. The same happens to the ice in any glacier tongues that try to invade these valleys. As a result, glaciers come to an abrupt stop without the melt stream normally found at their snouts. The valleys initially became so dry because the mountains held back the icecap. They are kept dry by the katabatic winds that accumulate on the icecap and rush down through the valleys. These high-speed winds are cold and very dry, with a humidity of less than 10 percent, and they suck away any moisture, making the valleys one of the driest places on Earth.

Visiting the Dry Valleys is the nearest humans may ever get to walking on the surface of Mars. Before they launched the Viking Probe towards that planet, scientists from NASA tested out their vehicles in the valleys. For geologists, the area provides a marvellous window into Antarctica's past. Previous glaciation has dug a hole into history and the dry winds and lack of streams mean that the rocks have lain perfectly preserved for thousands of years. Some rocks, though, have been eroded by the wind into extraordinary shapes known as ventifacts. These natural sculptures are so polished, curved and fluted that they look almost like an open air exhibition of Henry Moore's work. Even stranger are the bodies of crabeater seals among the rocks, almost perfectly mummified by the freeze-drying power of the wind. Some of the corpses are up to 80 kilometres from the sea and have probably been lying in the valleys for 3000 years.

Since the valleys are so dry and so cold, with temperatures dropping to minus 80 degrees centigrade in the winter, they might be expected to be as lifeless as the surface of the planet Mars they so resemble. But, as so often in the Antarctic, there are some creatures that can exist even there, though they are not obvious at first. Cracking open a porous rock with a geological hammer may reveal, just a few millimetres from the surface, a thin line of white, green or black. The white is a fungus, the green is an alga, the black a lichen, living in the interstices within the rock where they are protected from extreme desiccation.

Life inside rocks is not the only surprise in the Dry Valleys. Despite their name and nature, they contain a number of lakes and the only watercourse in Antarctica

PREVIOUS PAGE Hidden among the Transantarctic Mountains, the Dry Valleys remain free of ice and snow all year round.

RIGHT Powerful winds blow through the Dry Valleys picking up sand and gradually eroding the rocks into beautiful natural sculptures called ventifacts.

ABOVE In the autumn, just as the rest of the Antarctic's wildlife is heading north, emperor penguins start to appear at the ice edge and march south to their traditional nest sites on the sea ice.

LEFT Emperor penguins dive deeper than any other bird and have reached a remarkable 458 metres. The trails behind these birds are air bubbles released from their feathers by changing water pressure.

worthy of the title 'river'. The Onyx River starts outside the valleys as a melt stream from the Wright Glacier and extends for 40 kilometres through the Wright Valley. During most of the year it does not flow but for just a few weeks each summer it reaches an impressive enough size to make it difficult to ford. The Onyx flows into Lake Vanda, which is several kilometres long and permanently covered by 4 metres of ice. This largest and strangest of the Antarctic's lakes seems to operate as a giant solar heater. The Onyx is constantly depositing small quantities of salts in the lake which sink to the bottom and concentrate. Less salty water settles above the densest, saltiest water in layers with the least dense layer near the top. The permanent covering of ice on top of the lake keeps the layers stable. The ice has crystals arranged vertically in perfect rows and these transmit the heat of the sun down to the bottom of the lake. Because the water in the lake is layered and does not circulate, the heat stays at the bottom, which gradually warms up. So although the water near Lake Vanda's icy surface is always practically freezing, the temperature at the bottom of the lake can reach 25 degrees centigrade. The result is another unique niche for life. At various levels in the lake live different algae, bacteria and protozoans, each having chosen the temperature or density of salts that suits its particular make-up.

Above the Dry Valleys and held back by the Transantarctic Mountains is the great icecap of East Antarctica, over 3000 metres high. The altitude produces bitter conditions all year round, with temperatures averaging minus 30 degrees centigrade in the middle of summer and falling to at least minus 60 degrees centigrade during the winter. The world's lowest ever temperature, minus 89.6 degrees centigrade, was recorded in East Antarctica at the Russian station at Vostok, which sits at 3488 metres, higher even than the South Pole station. The two icecaps of East and West Antarctica between them cover 14 million square kilometres. Nowhere else on Earth can make people feel so totally insignificant as this high polar plateau. The landscape is just featureless white ice with only the odd brave peak, or nunatak, appearing above it. On these tiny havens of bare rock in a frozen desert there are outposts of life, tiny lichens sheltering in cracks and the occasional invertebrate. In the summer, skuas venture on to the icecap and snow petrels and Antarctic petrels may nest on nunataks near the coast. But during the long darkness of the winter, nothing moves on the Antarctic plateau.

In winter, the snow petrels can only be found hundreds of kilometres to the north on the edge of the sea ice. Though much of the Antarctic's wildlife escapes to the very fringes of the Southern Ocean, and in the case of some whales to more temperate seas, a stalwart few remain close to the ice edge. They tend to be species like the Adélie penguin and snow petrel that have a natural affinity for pack ice. Until recently, very few people had visited them in their winter home. Apart from the appalling winter weather, the edge of the ice is a frighteningly unpredictable place to be. Fringing the more permanent sea ice, there is always a region of pack ice which comes and goes with the wind. Long cracks or leads will suddenly break up previously firm ice and all round the continent there are permanent openings in the ice called polynias. But the advent of high-powered icebreakers has allowed researchers to go deep in the sea ice, right through the winter, and they have discovered that wherever there is open water, there is often life.

Minke and southern bottlenosed whales have been reported in the winter pack and they even turn up in polynias kilometres from open water. To reach these the whales must swim for a very long time under the ice without air. When they find an open polynia, the whales spend many minutes at the surface deep breathing, repaying the oxygen debt to their body tissues. Groups of killer whales are thought to have spent a complete winter living in a polynia, unable to return to the open ocean. But the animal that probably relies on these windows in the ice more than any other is the emperor penguin which has been known to walk 280 kilometres to reach a polynia. Emperors can dive deeper than any other bird and the polynias give them access to a deep-sea world largely unaffected by the harsh conditions above. Though they do take krill, the emperors' main foods are squid and, particularly, fish, and they have been recorded going as deep as 458 metres to catch their prey. On a single foraging trip they will make on average 100 dives, many of which are deeper than 200 metres. Humans diving to such depths would have their lungs crushed by the pressure. Nobody knows exactly how the penguins survive, nor how they catch their prey in complete darkness.

In early April, when the sea ice is starting to form again and most of the Antarctic's life is escaping north, the emperor penguins head south. They suddenly appear on the ice edge, shooting out of the ocean at great speed and pulling themselves up to their full height. As temperatures drop, the birds march south across the forming sea ice to their traditional nesting sites. The emperors are everything their name suggests, proud imperial penguins that seem altogether superior to their smaller, squabbling cousins. They stand over a metre tall, weigh 30 to 40 kilograms, and are as big as a man round the chest. At first sight they resemble king penguins with a blue-black back and wings and a white shirt-front shading into yellow above with orange ear patches. But the emperors weigh twice as much as the kings and have adopted a very different and truly remarkable life style. Breaking all the rules that govern other life in the Antarctic, they lay their eggs on ice in the deep south at the end of autumn and incubate them throughout the winter. This allows their chicks to hatch early in the spring and have

ABOVE AND RIGHT *In winter,
male emperor penguins huddle
together to conserve body heat.
The huddle is constantly on the
move and each bird takes his turn
at the exposed windward side.*

FOLLOWING PAGE *With
temperatures below minus 30
centigrade and wind speeds of up
to 200 kilometres per hour,
emperor penguins journey across
the sea ice to reach their colony.*

the whole summer, when food supplies are at their optimum, to grow to maturity. But for the parents the strategy involves what must be the greatest feat of survival in the natural world.

The total number of emperor penguins is unknown because new colonies are still being discovered, but there may be 135 000–175 000 pairs breeding in some 40 sites round the Antarctic continent. All the colonies are in the deep south between 66 and 78 degrees South, usually on areas of predictable fast ice. Some emperor colonies contain over 20 000 pairs and these look particularly impressive when all the birds are assembled on a flat open expanse of frozen sea ice for courting. Often this amphitheatre is surrounded by ice cliffs or gigantic icebergs. The penguins choose such places because they may offer a little protection from the worst of the winter winds. Emperor courtship is a noisy business with birds bowing and trumpeting at each other. Their songs are critical because during the winter the pairs will not have individual territories and each bird must recognize its mate by its particular song.

The female lays a single egg in early May and almost immediately passes it to her mate. The male is instinctively keen to take on his responsibility and wrestles with her for the precious burden. The emperor does not make a nest but keeps the egg carefully balanced in a brood pouch just above the feet. The egg is held against a patch of highly vascularised bare skin on the lower belly and a loose fold of skin on the bird's abdomen rolls down to completely encase it. It is essential that the egg does not freeze solid and in the depths of winter, the temperature inside the pouch may be 80 degrees centigrade higher than that outside. Once the male has the egg, the female leaves to spend the next 65 days at sea. The male must incubate the egg alone, spending much of his time in total darkness, being battered by katabatic winds that may reach 300 kilometres per hour. Temperatures may drop below minus 60 degrees centigrade, so cold that humans would find survival totally impossible whatever they were wearing. In addition, from the time he arrives on the ice the male emperor spends 115 days without a meal, a record fast for any bird. During his lonely vigil, the male loses 200 grams a day and if he makes it through the winter, he will be half his weight at courtship.

Emperors are highly adapted to endure the Antarctic winter. Of vital importance is a thick layer of blubber which both insulates the bird and provides energy during its fast. The feathers are closely packed and bent over at the bottom so that one lies on top of another, giving a layer four feathers thick. Each feather varies along its shaft from down at the bottom to waterproof and almost scaly at the tip to provide excellent protection from the cold. The exposed feet and bill are especially small to reduce heat

Until emperor penguin chicks are seven or eight weeks old
they are kept and fed in their parents' brood pouch.

loss. The nasal chambers in the beak recover much of warmth normally lost in breathing, while in the feet and flippers the arteries and veins lie close together so that the blood is warmed as it returns from these extremities. The emperor's adaptations are so effective that in summer, when the temperature climbs to nearly freezing, the birds overheat. Yet in the depths of winter the males cannot rely on their own bodies alone and must co-operate.

Most penguins are highly territorial birds and guard their own space aggressively. But male emperors will only make it through the winter if they overcome this natural aggression and huddle together for warmth. Thousands of penguins squeeze together in a single scrum of sheltering bodies and any individual that fails to join is sure to die. Packed tightly together, such a group of penguins can cut heat loss by 50 percent. Within the group, the birds co-operate further by taking it in turns to occupy the coldest, most exposed position. Particularly during the frequent blizzards, this is the windward side of the huddle. The group is constantly shifting as the birds taking the brunt of the wind gradually shuffle to the leeward side so that all the birds spend their fair share in the cold. During a two-day blizzard, the huddle may move by 200 metres in a slow-motion cascade. Occasionally two birds will have a squabble, sticking their heads up to peck at each other, and the commotion will ripple through the whole huddle. Suddenly all the males will raise their heads up and a great shimmer of warm air will rise from the colony, providing ample evidence for the value of their extraordinary co-operative behaviour.

Very few people have ever seen an emperor penguin huddle in winter. Those that have speak of a savage and lonely wilderness where ice and cold are king and only

After about eight weeks, emperor penguin chicks are too large for their parents' brood pouch and often have to huddle together to keep warm.

an emperor can endure. Huddled in silence, the penguins spend days of total darkness in temperatures cold enough to crack the teeth. Sometimes the darkness is broken by a spectacle that stopped the early explorers in their tracks. The sky is lit from edge to edge with curtains of ghostly lights, red and violet and green. The Maori people of New Zealand call this display *Tahu-Nui-A-Rangi*, 'the great burning of the sky', but it is better known elsewhere as aurora australis or the southern lights. It is caused by charged particles in the sun's powerful solar wind entering the Earth's atmosphere and interacting with the Earth's magnetic field to cause enormous electrical storms. In the Antarctic's black winter sky, the southern lights can be brighter than the moon, filling the whole sky with vibrating colours for many hours. Then this enormous television screen switches off and leaves the emperors once more in winter darkness.

In mid-July, usually just as the eggs are hatching in the males' brood pouch, the females return. The sea ice is then nearly at its fullest extent and the females must walk up to 100 kilometres over the ice in near permanent darkness. Though the sun has started on its journey to the southern hemisphere, the huddles of males still only see an hour or two of distant daylight each day. Each male is desperately awaiting his mate's return because he has nearly reached the end of his endurance. If the egg hatches before the female arrives, he can sustain the chick for 10 to 15 days by regurgitating a milky secretion from his gullet. But soon he will be forced to abandon the chick and head to sea to save himself.

On arrival at the colony, each female sings at the top of her voice to find her mate in the gloom. Once the pair are reunited, the female feeds the chick while it is still snug in the male's pouch and then he reluctantly passes the chick to her. This exchange has to be achieved in just 10 seconds as a chick exposed to the winter weather and ice for longer than two minutes will die. Relieved of their charges, the males make the long journey north to the open sea. Compared with the clean and fat returning females, they make a motley crew. Many of them are dangerously thin and their bellies are dirty, but still they retain the imperial demeanour of their breed. Boating along on their bellies or walking together in purposeful lines, the males reach their destination in two days if they keep going round the clock.

They leave a colony of females in full song. Like the courting pair, it is essential that chick and mother learn to recognize each other's song so that they can locate each other if they become separated. Bending right down so that her beak is within centimetres of her chick, the emperor calls with all her might and the chick responds with ear-piercing whistles. The mother keeps the chick in her pouch and feeds it on demand for just over three weeks. Then her mate returns, revived by his time at sea, and takes over responsibility for the chick again. While being passed from pouch to pouch, the chick may be in danger from more than just the cold. Many males fail to survive the rigours of winter and their mates return to find themselves without a partner or a chick. These so-called maverick birds have such strong maternal instincts that they search desperately through the colony for any chick outside a brood pouch and scoop it up immediately. But weeks later, when the maverick female fails to be relieved by the male she lost in winter, she is forced to abandon the chick and return to sea. Six percent of all chick deaths are caused by this behaviour.

By seven or eight weeks of age, the emperor penguin chick weighs 2 kilograms and is too large for the brood pouch. At this stage, it can only be described as cute. If a soft-toy designer wanted a model for the ultimate cuddly toy, the emperor chick would have to be the strongest candidate in nature. The weather so early in the season is still very cold and spring brings many storms. The chicks are forced to huddle like their parents and many will perish before the summer. The parents meanwhile struggle to and from the ice edge to forage. The distance they must cover is so great that during

the full breeding season they can only manage about fourteen trips between them. However, each meal may be as much as 30 percent of the chick's weight and by five months of age the young weigh almost 15 kilograms. Then the parents are forced to leave their chicks and return to the sea to build up their strength to moult. Within three months the adults will have moulted and will begin their breeding cycle once again.

A week after their parents leave, the chicks, driven by hunger, follow them to the ice edge. This is coming closer all the time as the sea ice breaks up. Indeed, a major threat facing the emperors is that the sea ice will melt under the colony before the young are ready to leave. The emperor penguin chicks must be able to take their first swim in the Southern Ocean just five months after hatching. This fledging takes place in December when there are still a few months of summer remaining with lots of food to keep them growing. King penguin chicks, on the other hand, take 10 to 13 months to fledge and must be fed by their parents throughout the winter. So the kings need access to the sea all year round, restricting their breeding to the sub-Antarctic islands to the north.

It is fascinating that birds as similar as the king and emperor penguins have adopted such different breeding strategies that they hardly ever meet. While the king penguin's strategy only allows it to have two offspring every three years, the emperor's unique ability to lay its eggs on ice allows it to rear a chick every year. But the rigours of the deep south mean that while 80 percent of king penguin chicks will survive their first year, only 19 percent of emperor chicks will make it through. The contrast between the approaches to survival of these two birds is just one of the many enigmas of the Antarctic uncovered through the patient work of small groups of scientists over the last few decades.

The southern lights, aurora australis, light up the black of the winter sky above a base on White Island on the Ross Ice Shelf.

CHAPTER EIGHT

FOOTSTEPS IN THE SNOW

T HE MALE emperor penguin's extraordinary act of endurance takes place on the fringes of the continent, almost at sea level. For all its severity, the winter there is softened slightly by the Southern Ocean, which is at most only a metre or two below the penguins. Inland, the continent climbs 3000 metres or more to the high polar plateau. At its highest point, the average temperature is minus 60 degrees centigrade. Snow continually drifts over the crevassed ice sheet, blown by persistent winds. In winter, a few mites and lichens cling to life in sheltered corners of isolated nunataks, waiting for the return of the sun to re-activate, but no animal moves, no bird flies. No species managed to survive the winter while remaining active in this harshest of deserts – until 1957. Then humans, alone among the animal kingdom, had the audacity to try and live on the great Antarctic icecap.

We are not particularly well suited to the cold, as scientists who have observed the emperors in winter would attest. While the emperors withstand months of exposure, human observers dressed in many layers of thermal clothes can only tolerate being out with them for about half an hour at a time. We lack the layer of blubber possessed by most Antarctic mammals. Nor do we have the thick protective feathers or fur that give additional protection to the emperor penguin and Weddell seal on the edge of the continent. At the super cold temperatures reached in the interior, such as the Vostok record of minus 86.9 degrees centigrade, unprotected human flesh freezes in moments and lungs can be damaged by careless breathing. Any metal object grasped will stick to

Man meets emperor penguin in a vast lonely wilderness of pack ice.

the hand and tear off skin if removed. So humans can only survive there by constructing some form of shelter that will insulate them from the worst of the weather.

The first base, or station, on the icecap was not built until many decades after the great geographical prize of the South Pole had been won. In the interim, various countries claimed pie-shaped segments of Antarctica. In an age when major powers were carving up the world between them, such claims were inevitable and none was vigorously pursued. Unlike hotly disputed lands, Antarctica offered no possibility of permanent settlements and no easily exploitable resources. A fear of German expansion into the Antarctic produced a brief flurry of political and military activity in the region during the Second World War. And after the war, Antarctica might have become a minor pawn in the battle between the United States and the Soviet Union. But gradually, science began to hold sway over politics.

During the first half of this century, some bases were built on the periphery of the Antarctic and a number of expeditions were mounted. These included detailed surveys of some areas and, in 1935, the first flight over Antarctica. Wartime developments in transport and communications made exploration of the Antarctic more feasible. Also, several countries had surplus military personnel after the war. The United States launched huge operations in Antarctica, one of which involved 4700 servicemen, 13 ships and 51 scientists. But by the early 1950s, Antarctica still retained most of its secrets maybe because about half of the continent had not even been seen by human eyes.

Then a core of 12 nations agreed to focus a huge scientific effort on Antarctica in what became known as the International Geophysical Year 1957–58. This resulted in the first intercontinental flights to Antarctica, by the United States; the first journey to the south geomagnetic pole, by the Soviet Union; and the first land crossing of the continent, by the British Commonwealth Trans-Antarctic Expedition. By 1958, vastly more was known about Antarctica and its importance to the planet, and 35 bases had been established. An even more important breakthrough occurred in 1961 when the Antarctic Treaty was signed. This neither accepted nor rejected any of the various territorial claims that had been made on Antarctica. Instead the signatories, which to date number 40 nations, agreed that the continent would be devoted to scientific research. Scientists from any treaty nation can work there freely, provided their research is for peaceful purposes and does not exploit or harm any of the continent's plants and animals. It was later agreed that there would be no exploitation of mineral resources for at least 50 years. Antarctica's isolation was over and it had become, uniquely, a continent for science.

Even in the summer it is so cold at the South Pole that your
breath immediately freezes the front of your balaclava.

Today, the number of people who go to the Antarctic each year is still less than would occupy a small town. After more than 40 years of concentrated scientific exploration, there are 25 permanent stations on the main part of the continent, 12 on the Peninsula and nearby islands, and a further 20 on sub-Antarctic islands. In the height of summer, these bases are home to about 3500 scientists and ancillary staff. Their numbers are swelled intermittently by the crews of the transport delivering food and fuel, stores and supplies, and all the staff and scientists needed to operate the stations for the next year. Some bases are reached by intercontinental flight, but most rely upon strengthened, ice-breaking ships which come from South America, Asia and further afield. The ships and aircraft also bring 3000–4000 visitors to the Antarctic. Some of these, like the early explorers, wish to pit themselves against the mighty continent. A larger group, fired by the explorers' accounts, come to Antarctica as tourists. It is as expensive to transport a tourist as a scientist so the price-tag of such holidays is high but the experience is unforgettable. Well-managed tourists make excellent ambassadors for Antarctica and have provoked much new interest in the region.

Like the birds and the seals, the ships and aircraft are forced north in autumn, taking the tourists and other visitors with them. Many scientists, too, break camp, pack up and leave. As autumn progresses, the final ship calls are made, bringing the last opportunity to post mail for months, and the start of the winter period for the 1500 or less people overwintering at the bases. Those remaining have some slight regrets, but also excitement at the thought of the big freeze ahead, winter storms, isolation and the realization that there is now no way out.

The period of isolation is shortest for those in bases on the sub-Antarctic islands, such as that on Bird Island, just off the north-west coast of South Georgia. This base accommodates eight or nine scientists in summer, dropping to three or so in winter. The occupants never have less than several hours of sunlight a day but even in summer, it is no place for sun-seekers. Caught in the great swirling weather systems of the Southern Ocean, Bird Island is subject to cloud and rain, and most days have a damp and foggy start. The base is hardly visible as you approach by sea, obscured not by cloud but by a prominent headland that shelters the site from the worst of the weather. A small scaffold jetty provides a landing where you are met by a cheerful scientist leaning on a stout staff. As he escorts you the hundred or so metres to the two main base buildings, the reason for the staff becomes apparent because although the site has been used by people off and on for more than 30 years, other inhabitants have a prior claim to the beach. From the safety of the main hut, through its picture windows, you can

Tourists are ferried by Zodiac from their cruise ship
to a gentoo penguin colony along the Antarctic Peninsula.

look out on to a beach full of fur seals (who have notoriously sharp teeth) and marvel how you reached the hut unscathed.

The job of the scientists on Bird Island is not to explore the area but, equally wearing physically, to spend long days in the field studying albatrosses, petrels and seals. In the winter, most of these animals are at sea and only the wandering albatross chicks remain. The researchers leave the base in the morning, equipped with a thermos and lunch, to face a hard slog across icy tussock clumps and the inevitable tumbles into snow-filled gaps between. The fur seal's summer battlegrounds are hidden by snow, and on still, cold days the water in the bay grows a thin film of ice only to be destroyed by the next wind. On reaching the nesting areas, the researchers observe the chicks during the brief hours of winter light and then return for long evenings at the base.

Throughout the year, the scientists receive data on the movements of the albatrosses and seals. Signals from minute radio transmitters on the animals' backs are sent via satellite to ground stations in France. From there, they pass through high-speed data links to the headquarters in Britain and then back by satellite to the Antarctic. A research ship off South Georgia can receive the exact location of a particular bird within hours of its passing. The seals also bear pressure sensitive tags that reveal the depth to which they dive. The tags have changed scientists' perspective on seals. They were thought of as surface animals which dive for food and occasionally come ashore to breed. Now work at South Georgia has shown that the elephant seal lives most of its life at a depth of 400–600 metres, returning occasionally to the surface to breathe and, much more rarely, to the beach to breed.

The enormous amount of data needed to build up a clear picture of the lives of the birds and seals means that in the main hut lap-top computers and field notebooks vie for space with piles of research papers and scientific equipment. In addition to research duties, the scientists must maintain the equipment, and fit in cooking, cleaning and all other base chores. The living quarters are comfortable and secure, with a range for cooking and heating in the middle. There is also a small generator housed in a separate building, which is usually only run during the evening or when somebody is working in the base during the day. The power supply charges batteries and runs freezers, video machines and a whole host of scientific equipment. Plumbing is more spartan and relies on a small plastic pipe from a nearby dammed stream. Since dying fur seals have no respect for this water supply, it cannot be drunk and crates of bottled water are delivered by ship each summer.

For those on a base, 'summer' is judged to be the time between the arrival of

During the winter the tiny British Antarctic Survey base on Bird Island
is home to just three people.

the first ship with fresh supplies and the departure of the last ship, and this period becomes much shorter further south. In the maritime Antarctic and on the edge of the continent, sea ice makes access impossible for much of the year. Stations on the Peninsula may not see a ship for eight or nine months, while those on the edge of the high plateau, such as Mawson, can be isolated for ten or eleven months. Mawson was opened in February 1954 on an isolated group of rocks just 300 kilometres from Scullin Monolith. Another outcrop almost smothered by ice, Scullin is thick with thousands of breeding petrels during the short summer. Mawson is home to about 50 people in summer and about half that number during the long winter.

Stations such as Mawson need powerful generators to provide constant heat and light. These add to the danger of fire, which is feared by base staff almost more than the cold. The humidity in the Antarctic is very low, particularly in winter when nearly all the moisture is locked up in ice. A tiny spark can ignite tinder dry wood and paper, and a fire spreads quickly in the near constant winds. In every station, a routine fire patrol checks the buildings while the rest of the staff are asleep. A fire in winter, with no hope of replacement shelter or stores for months, could spell disaster. So each station has a small building set to one side, stocked with food, fuel, tents and a radio in case the worst should happen. It has, several times, sadly with some loss of life.

Other major challenges for those overwintering are the darkness and isolation. After the last ship has gone, the seas around Mawson gradually choke with icebergs from nearby glacier fronts, frozen together by winter ice. The sun arches lower in the sky each day and the light fades into a permanent gloom. Creeping along the horizon, intermittently hidden behind icebergs, the sun is lost to one final tilt of the Earth. Then an afterglow in the northern sky fades to leave a permanent night, which lasts for just a few weeks at this latitude. The long hours of darkness and the restrictions on activities around a base, imposed for the safety of staff, generate tensions. With no dawn or dusk, getting up in the 'morning' becomes increasingly hard, going to bed worse and a weariness clouds every eye. This is the most testing time for the staff at Mawson and the other 1500 or so humans overwintering in the Antarctic. They cope with the isolation partly through keeping busy. This is not difficult since the high cost of running an Antarctic station means that none is overstaffed. Everyone has to help with the general base chores, such as cleaning the floors, fetching snow for water and moving supplies under shelter. Also crucial is the ability to get along with and co-operate with the small pool of individuals at the base. With so few people scattered over millions of square kilometres, there is little prospect of visits from the neighbours.

Eventually the social event of the Antarctic year, the midwinter party, comes

In the winter months Antarctica's only light comes from the generators on scientific bases.

LEFT *The Australian base at Mawson is built on one of the rare patches of bare rock on the edge of Antarctica. During the summer about 20 scientists and about 30 support staff work here. For the winter, numbers drop below 20 and only two or three of those are scientists.*

ABOVE *A wandering albatross chick is weighed as part of a long term study of their breeding and feeding ecology that has been undertaken by the British Antarctic Survey on Bird Island, South Georgia. These chicks are the largest of any seabird with a record weight of 17 kilogrammes.*

to break the tedium. Every base joins the party, like an individual candle in the Antarctic cake. Telegrams fly to all corners of the world, proclaiming undying fraternity. There is a sumptuous dinner, and the celebrations, including pantomimes, ice races and radio darts matches, continue for a week. The promise of the sun's return lifts everyone's spirits, but probably the most relieved are those staff in the select group of bases that operate year round on the Antarctic icecap.

The first stations in the heart of Antarctica were built in 1957 by the United States and the Soviet Union as part of the International Geophysical Year effort. The costs are so great that no other nations have yet joined them, although recently the French have proposed doing so. The expense can be gauged from the 176 transporter flights needed each year to service the United States' Amundsen-Scott base at the South Pole. The Russian Vostok base, at the south geomagnetic pole, is re-supplied by tractor trail from a coastal base over 1300 kilometres away. Tractor trains kilometres long take several weeks to complete the journey, bringing stores and the 25 to 30 people destined to run the station through the next winter.

Such is the shortage of suitable rock sites around the continent that many stations have been built directly on the ice. At the edge of the continent, where snowfall is high and near-continuous winds pile great drifts, bases must be constructed to withstand being buried. At some sites, people have lived as moles, descending 9 or 10 metre ladders to reach the warmth of their huts. Eventually, the forces in the ice smash the buildings, no matter how strong they are. But on the Antarctic icecap, temperatures are so low that snow does not readily form. So the groups of men and women who work in the terrible conditions on the high polar plateau are at least spared sub-ice living quarters.

It was in 1957, 45 years after Amundsen's and Scott's expeditions, that the next human footprints appeared at the South Pole. They were made by a United States crew who had stepped out of an aeroplane to build a station at the pole, at an elevation of 2835 metres. Rebuilt in 1975, the station caters for 100 scientists and technical staff in summer, and about 20 during the winter. A 17 metre high geodesic dome houses prefabricated living quarters, a galley, scientific buildings, a communications centre, a post office and a library. Beside the dome is a five storey sky-lab tower with a large picture-windowed lounge at the top. The lounge is very popular all year, especially during winter when brilliant auroras can be seen.

The Amundsen-Scott base cost millions of dollars to build but the spectacular auroral displays provide a clue to why the money was well spent. The daily movements of the auroras give valuable information about the Earth's magnetic field. In addition,

A Hercules aircraft comes in to land on the sea ice in front of the Royal Society Range.

astronomers have moved from city to countryside to oceanic island in search of a clear view of the heavens away from polluted air and the glow of electric lights. The South Pole offers six months of total darkness and clean air free from dust. It is one of the few places in the world where high-energy radiation from space, such as gamma rays, can be studied. The South Pole observatory also monitors the atmosphere's ozone layer, which shields us from much of the sun's harmful ultraviolet radiation. Some of the gases we have manufactured and released into the air are damaging the ozone layer, and this is particularly noticeable above the Antarctic. Scientists gather data about the damage by recording the amount of ultraviolet radiation reaching the pole.

During the summer, the researchers at the high polar plateau bases try to find out more about the continent and its thick cover of ice. Some fly for hours in small cramped aircraft over the seemingly endless icecap. Among the more puzzling features they have observed are the five vast ice streams, one 50 kilometres across, that flow from the icecap of West Antarctica into the Ross Ice Shelf. Ice streams are just like glaciers, except that they flow through slow-moving ice instead of between mountains. Those that flow into the Ross Ice Shelf move unusually fast and upstream from them are strange depressions in the ice sheet. One of the depressions is 50 metres deep and several kilometres long. Using radio waves and other remote sensing techniques, scientists have built up a rough picture of what lies under the ice. This shows that below the depression there appears to be a peak, which looks like the caldera of a volcano, rising to within 1400 metres of the surface of the icecap.

From this and other data, scientists suspect that an active, or recently active, volcano exists beneath the ice at nearly 82 degrees South. If so, it will be the most southerly of several active volcanoes around the Antarctic. By making assumptions about the state and size of the volcano, researchers estimate that it generates about 700 megawatts of power, equivalent to a medium-sized power station and enough to melt about two-thirds of a cubic kilometre of ice a year. It may be that water from the melting ice provides the lubricant for the fast-flowing ice streams nearby. Nobody can go beneath the icecap to confirm any of these suppositions. But drilling deep into one of the ice streams produced ice cores with wet, fine glacial clay at the bottom, an ideal substrate for ice to slide on.

While ideas about what is below the icecap have to be largely guesswork, scientists can investigate the pack ice at first hand. Lying between the fast ice round the continent and the open ocean beyond, the 200 kilometre or more wide pack-ice zone is believed to play an important role in the absorption of carbon dioxide by the polar

Scientists launch a balloon as part of a study into the hole in the ozone layer which was first discovered over Antarctica.

ocean in winter. It is also thought to help in the formation and break-up of Antarctic sea ice, and to act as a winter source of food for many penguins, petrels and seals. So knowledge about the zone is crucial.

The pack ice used to be a serious barrier but now ships have been built with the power and strength to match the forces in it. During the early Antarctic spring of 1992, two such ships journeyed to the pack ice off the west coast of the Antarctic Peninsula. One stayed in the open ocean while the other sailed as far as it could into the ice. Then both stayed in place, using satellite data to fix their positions, as the returning sun gradually reduced the extent of the ice. The 40 or so scientists on board the inner ship studied the changes in the pack as the ice retreated past. Divers measured the activity of animals and plants under the ice, while echo-sounders detected unexpected numbers of krill swarms below and sea-ice scientists worked on large icefloes near the ship. All this activity was just part of a major international research project. Scientists of one nation could not afford to investigate the vast area of the pack. Only by pooling the resources of many nations can we hope to uncover this region's secrets.

Terra Australis Incognita was a great disappointment to the early explorers. If it had been the green and fertile place they hoped for, Antarctica would doubtless have been fought over and transformed by the victors. But even exploring the ice-locked land they found has demanded great ingenuity, courage – and money. So those who want to find out more about the continent are forced, like the emperor penguins, to co-operate to achieve their aims. The collaborative work set in motion in the 1950s has shown that Antarctica is vital to the health of the planet. It also has most of the world's fresh water frozen into a protective layer over mineral-rich rocks. Fortunately, these precious resources cannot yet be exploited economically, and Antarctica remains virtually unscathed. There is a proposal, still being considered, that the whole continent should be declared a World Wilderness Park. Whatever its status, it is to be hoped that this sole remaining pristine continent continues to be a place where human footsteps are gentle and infrequent.

PREVIOUS PAGE Evening light on mountains of the Antarctic Peninsula.
This is the entrance to The Gullet at the top of Marguerite Bay.

INDEX